ART OF WRITING

فـن الـكتابة

By

Ibrahim A. S. Abu- Anza

*****

تـأليـف

إبــراهـيـم عـبـدالـرحـيـم أبـوعـنـزه

*****

2006

Art Of Writing

فـن الكتـابـة

1st Edition 2003

2nd Edition 2006

بــسـم اللـه الـرحـمـن الرحـيـم

قـال اللـه تـعـالى فـي سـورة الـروم :

" ومـن آيـاتـه خـلـقُ الـسـماواتِ والأرض واخـتـلافُ
ألـسنتكـم وألـوانـكم . إنَّ في ذلك لآيـاتٍ للعالِـمـين."

Allah says that of His signs are the creation of the heavens and the diversity of your languages and colours . These are signs for people who know.

⋈⋈⋈⋈⋈⋈⋈⋈⋈

وقـال تـعـالى :

" إنـما يـخـشى اللـهَ مـن عبادهِ العلـماء. "

Allah says that of His human creatures learned ones fear Him."

قـال سيِّـدنـا محـمد عليه الصلاة والسلام :

" مـن تـعـلَّم لغـةَ قـومٍ أمِـنَ مكْرَهـم ."

The prophet , Muhammad (PBUH) , says that he who learns the language of another community will be safe from their treachery .

3

Introduction

People use language to communicate with each other in different ways. One way of communication is writing , a language skill that is not easy to acquire. To communicate well through writing is not an easy job. You need a lot of permanent practice. But to be able to write well , you have to meet certain requirements. First, you should possess a reasonable amount of English vocabulary . Second , you should be familiar with the basics of the English grammar so that you can use vocabulary in making sentences that can communicate your ideas to others , thus reaching sound communication. Third , you need to read a lot ;you have to read others' writings so as to develop your writing skill. You benefit a lot from what others have written ; you can see new ideas expressed in language you need to imitate .

This book provides practical solutions to writing problems ; many students complain that they do not know how to write . They complain that they do not have clear ideas of the topic they have to write about. The other problem is being unable to produce the appropriate language that expresses ideas if they have them.

The book addresses these problems providing the learner with practical ways that enable him (her) to develop the writing skill. The point worth mentioning is the fact that the writing skill is not innate; one acquires it through diligent practice and through reading. There is nothing wrong with learning certain expressions that you can use when dealing with different topics . You can borrow others' language when writing about another topic making some necessary changes .

The book contains some useful writing tips , some common expressions , some grammatical points and key vocabulary. The book shows a variety of compositions expressing different topics. The aim is to let you read the composition so as to learn something from it . Try to imitate it by using the same language after you have modified it so as to serve your purpose.

The book gives the Arabic meanings of words used in every composition with an attempt to provide an approximate pronunciation in Arabic of some words .

I am fully confident that this book , if given due consideration ,will relieve students by improving their writing skill.

The author : Ibrahim Abu Anza

Doha 2006

مقـــدمـــة

يسرني أن أقدّم هذا الكتاب – فن الكتابة – لتقديم حلول عملية للمشاكل التي يواجهها الطلاب عندما يريدون الكتابة عن موضوع ما . ومن المعروف أن التفاهم بين الناس يأخذ أشكالاً كثيرة منها الكتابة. والكتابة مهارة يتم اكتسابها عن طريق قراءة كتابات أناس آخرين وعن طريق الممارسة . وحتى تتمكن من الكتابة الجيدة , لا بد من توفر أمور ضرورية مثل حيازة قدر معقول من المفردات والإلمام بأساسيات قواعد اللغة الإنجليزية حتى يتمكن الدارس من معرفة كيفية استخدام الكلمة في بناء جملة تكون معبرة عن فكرة يريد الدارس توصيلها إلى الآخرين , ثم أن تقرأ ما كتبه الآخرون حتى تستفيد من أفكارهم و طريقة استخدام اللغة في التعبير .

إن القراءة أمر في غاية الأهمية لأنك تستطيع أن تستعير بعضاً من لغة الآخرين لكي تنمي أسلوبك حتى تتمكن من الوقوف على قدميك وعندها تكون قد طورت طريقةً وأسلوباً خاصين بك . إننا في هذه الحياة مقلدون للآخرين .... نرى تجاربهم لنتعلم منها .

إن هذا الكتاب يحتوي على مواضيع عديدة لا بأس أن تقرأها جيداً وخذ منها اللغة التي تراها جميلة بمعنى تلك اللغة التي تساعدك في التعبير عن موضوع أخر . وهناك نصائح تتعلق بكيفية اكتساب وتنمية مهارة الكتابة إذا ما طبقت . كما يقدّم الكتاب بعض القواعد النحوية التي بدونها لا يمكن تنمية هذه المهارة . كما يقدّم الكتاب بعد كل موضوع الكلمات الأساسية التي وردت في الموضوع ويعقب ذلك تمرين على المفردات الغاية منه إكساب الدارس القدرة على التعبير .
وهناك محاولة لنطق بعض الكلمات بالعربية حتى يسهل على الدارس حفظها . وإني على ثقة كبيرة بأن هذا الكتاب سوف يمكّن الدارسين من تجاوز صعوبة الكتابة إذا أعطى الدارسُ هذا الكتاب الاهتمام الذي يستحقه .

ويـسرني أن أقدّم الطبعة الثانية من هذا الكتاب بعد أن أدخلت الكثير من التعديلات والمواضيع الجديدة بلغة سهلة واسلوب يناسب كافة المستويات راجياً الله العلي القدير أن ينفع به العباد .

المؤلف : إبراهـــيم عبدالرحيم أبوعنـزه
الدوحة / يونـيه 2006

قواعد اللغة Grammar

To be a successful writer , a knowledge of English grammar is essential. We provide some grammar information without which one cannot embark on a successful writing task. This basically includes what is termed as parts of speech, which means that a word can be a noun or a verb or an adjective. It is important to know how a word is used in making a sound sentence that conveys an idea to others.

لكي يكون المرء ناجحاً في الكتابة , لا بد أن تتوفر لديه معرفة بقواعد اللغة الإنجليزية . ونقدّم بعض المعلومات المتعلقة بالقواعد وهذه تتضمن بصفة أساسية ما اصطلح على تسميته بأجزاء الكلام , ونعني بـذلك أن الكلمـة قـد تكـون اسمـاً أو فعلاً أو صفة. ومن المهم أن نعرف كيفية استخدام الكلمة في تكوين جملة سليمة توصل فكرة إلى الأخرين.

Parts of Speech   أجزاء الكلام
1- The noun :الاسم

Ali , Mona , Tom , Susan , Doha , Qatar , food , sports , السرعة speed , book , story قصة , business أعمال , money , freedom الحرية , smoking , milk , apples , trees, newspaper , plan خطة , project المشروع , wine الخمر , the Sun الشمس , the weather الجو , energy الطاقة , sports .

* هناك ضمائر تؤدي نفس دور الاسم وهذه الضمائر هي :

(هو – للفاعل) he,أنت- أنتما- أنتم – أنتِ you, أنا I
, her – للمفعول به , هي – للفاعل she   (هو – للمفعول به) him
هم – هن -(للفاعل) they / نحن- للمفعول به us / نحن – للفاعل (money أو book أو car) We / إنه -إنها- للفاعل والمفعول به It
.إنهم – إنها – إنهن   (للمفعول به)them

6

* **The function of the noun (pronoun)** وظيفة الاسم أو الضمير

The noun can function as a subject فاعل or an object مفعول به

الاسم يقوم بوظيفة فاعل أو مفعول به .

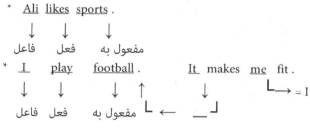

* <u>Ali</u> <u>likes</u> <u>sports</u> .

    ↓   ↓   ↓

فاعل   فعل   مفعول به

* <u>I</u> <u>play</u> <u>football</u> .   <u>It</u> makes <u>me</u> fit .   ∟→ = I

فاعل   فعل   مفعول به

* <u>Ali and Nasser</u> read many <u>books</u>.

      كثـيرة.   كتبـاً   إن عليـاً وناصراً يقـرآن

* <u>They</u> benefit a lot from <u>them</u> .   إنهما يستفيدا ن كثيراً منها

* This book is useful .   هذا الكتاب مفيد.
* Hamad is a pilot .   إن حمداً طيار .

      ↓   ↓

اسم في محل صفة للفاعل   / اسم في محل فاعل

* We are students .   نحن طلاب

      ↓   ↓

اسم في محل صفة للفاعل / ضمير في محل اسم

2- **The adjective** الصفة :

good طيب , polite مؤدب , nice لطيف, bad سئ ,
impolite غير مؤدب , rude وقح-فظ , dirty وسخ ,
ambitious طموح , hopeful متفائل , hopeless يائس ,

7

friendly , homeless مشرد , careless مهمل , careful حذر – منتبه

poor , rich غني , tolerant متسامح , wrong مخطئ , right محق , frank صريح ودود

mad مجنون , deep عميق , narrow ضيق , high عالٍ , sad حزين silly سخيف , فقير

low , expensive غا , cheap رخيص , dangerous خطير , useful مفيد , important مهم , منخفض

happy , young شاب – صغير السن , fresh طازج , tired متعب , angry غاضب , لٍ

سعيد .

* **How to use the adjective** كيفية استخدام الصفة :

* We use the adjective to describe the noun.

نستخدم الصفة لكي نصف الاسم .

* I am **happy** . إني سعيد

↓ ↓

صفة للاسم وهي خبر / ضمير في محل اسم (مبتدأ)

* I **am** careful and hopeful .

↓

هذا فعل يأتي بين الاسم والصفة

مثله مثل is , are

* I am **careful** , but Ali is **careless** .
* This man is **homeless** .
* You are **frank** .
* We are **ambitious.**
* This book is **useful** .
* These books are **important.**
* This car is **expensive** .
* The girls are **nice.**

* في اللغة العربية لا داعي لاستخدام فعل الكينونة بين المبتدأ والخبر (صفة المبتدأ) .

❖ I **am** sad . إني حزين
❖ Hamad **is** generous . حمد كريم
❖ You **are** rich . أنت غني
❖ The road **is** narrow and dark. الطريق ضيق ومظلم

❖ Some people **are** silly .　　　بعض الناس سخفاء

❖ Hamad　is **a generous man**.　　إن حمداً رجل كريم .

❖ **The small car** is cheap .　　السيارة الصغيرة رخيصة.

* **Fresh milk** is good for you.　الحليب الطازج يصلح لك.

* في الأمثلة الثلاثة الأخيرة نجد أن الصفة تسبق الاسم الموصوف:

a generous man , a small car , fresh milk .

* في الإنجليزية الصفة تبقى ثابتة سواء كان الاسم مذكراً أو مؤنثاً، مفرداً أو جمعاً.

❖ Ali　is **kind** . Mona is **kind** , too .

❖ Some people are **selfish** .　　بعض الناس أنانيون

❖ Nasser is **selfish**.

* ننصح بعمل جملٍ مماثلة متتبعين النموذج السابق مع استبدال صفة أخرى.

　3-　**The verb** الفعل :

play يلعب , pray يصلي , wash يغسل- يغتسل , watch يشاهد , visit يزور
help يساعد, save يوفر (مالاً)- ينقذ use يستخدم , speak يتكلم , read يقرأ , learn يتعلم ,
win يفوز بـ , lose يخسر , benefit from يستفيد من , suffer from يعاني من , respect يحترم
improve يتحسن-يحسّن, spoil يُفسد , change يتغير - يغير , fight يناضل - يكافح - يحارب
buy يشتري , use يستخدم , misuse يسيئ استخدام , destroy يدمر , solve يحل , relieve
drink , accept يقبل بـ, write يكتب , show يوضح - يُري - يُبرز - يُظهر , يخفف من معاناة
يشرب .

* **How to use the verb**　كيفية استخدام الفعل :

To use a verb for making a sentence , we have to follow

لاستخدام الفعل في تكوين جملة علينا أن نتبع هذا النمط : . this pattern

Noun (فاعل)اسم ⟶ فعل verb ⟶ noun (مفعول به)اسم

I	speak	English .
We	need	food and medicine.

* The verb has four forms , and you have to learn
to use each form.

* إن الفعل له أربعة أشكا ل وعليك أن تتعلم كيفية استخدام كل شكل.

إليك تصاريف بعض الأفعال :

1	2	3	4
play	played	played	playing
wash	washed	washed	washing
learn	learnt	learnt	learning
write	wrote	written	writing
see	saw	seen	seeing
get	got	got	getting
buy	bought	bought	buying
sell يبيع	sold	sold	selling

1-When to use the first verb :

متى نستخدم الشكل الأول للفعل

عادة نستخدم الشكل الأول للفعل عندما نريد أن نتحدث عن حقائق و أمور يعتاد على القيام بها في الحاضر.

* We **get** milk from cows. إننا نحصل على الحليب من الأبقار .
* Ali **gets** a good salary. إن علياً يحصل على راتب جيد.
* Mona **gets** everything from me.
* I **play** football .
* Ali **plays** basketball .
* I **don't play** basketball . إني لا ألعب كرة السلة .
* Ali **doesn't play** football.
* Mona **doesn't speak** French. إن منى لا تتكلم الفرنسية.
* Food **gives** people energy. * إن الطعام يمنح الناس طاقة. We **give** Ali everything.

* عليكم ملاحظة أن الفعل في الشكل الأول يكتسب إذا جاء الفاعل مثل علي أو منى او الطعام es / s

* في حالة النفي نستخدم **don't** أو **doesn't** مع الشكل الأول للفعل .

* يجب أن نتدرّب على تكوين جملٍ مماثلة باستخدام فعل جديد في كل مرة.

I have a brother and a sister . They are different.

I like Hamad because he is generous . Hamad helps poor people. He likes reading ,but he does not like noise . Hamad does not play football , but he plays chess. My sister , Noura, is different . She does not like reading. She thinks that reading is boring. Noura likes music so much.　　　　She spends too much time listening to it. I do not like that.　　　 I do not agree with her. I tell her that music is bad, but she is not ready to change her mind. I do not   know what to do. I need somebody to tell me what to do with my noisy sister.

****

* A lexical verb with an auxiliary الفعل مع فعل مساعد

We can use auxiliaries أفعال مساعدة to convey other ideas.

يمكننا أن نستخدم أفعال مساعدة مع الفعل لتوصيل أفكار أخرى

1- Ali **will** show a way .　　　　إن علياً سوف يريك طريقة.

2- I **can** show you the way to the park.

إني أستطيع أن أريك الطريق المؤدي ا لي الحديقة.

3-　He **cannot** help you.　　　　إنه لا يستطيع أن يساعدك.

4-　We **must** do something .　　　　يجب أن نفعل شيئاً.

5-　We **have to** solve the problem.　　　علينا أن نحل المشكلة.

6-　We **should** relieve people.　　　يجب علينا أن نخفف

من معاناة الناس.

الكلمات بالحبر الاسود الغامق هي **أفعال مساعدة بل مقويات للفعل** لأنها تساعدنا على التعبير عـن أفكار أخرى على صلة بالفكرة الأولى وهذا يعزز الفكرة الأولى لأننا نجد أمامنا سـبيلاً لأن نؤكد عليهـا بواسطة استخدام أشكال أخرى من الجمل.

* وهناك مقويات أخرى يمكننا الاستفادة منها عندما نريد أن نعبر عن نفس

11

الفكرة .

* I **want** to learn English.
* You **should** learn this important language.
* I **advise** you to learn English.

إني أنصحك
بأن تتعلم الإنجليزية.

* It is **important to** learn this language.

من المهم أن تتعلم .....

* It is **useful to** learn ....

من المفيد أن........

* It **is necessary to** ....

من الضروري أن ....

* يمكننا أن نستخدم التراكيب السابقة عندما نتحدث عن أمر أخر نؤيده. أما إذا كنا لا
نؤيد أمراً فيمكننا أن نستخدم بعضاً من التراكيب التالية .

* You **should not drink** wine.

يجب أن لا تشرب الخمر.

* I **don't advise** you to drink wine .

إني لا أنصحك
بأن تشرب الخمر.

* It **is wrong to** drink wine.

* It من الخطأ أن تشرب الخمر.

is **mad to** ....

* It is من الجنون أن ....

dangerous to ....

* It is shameful من الخطر أن ....

to ......

* ولكي ترغَّب الناس فيما   من العيب أن   ....

تدعو إليه , يمكنك الاستعانة بهذه التراكيب.

* I **advise** you to drink fresh milk.
* It is **useful to** drink fresh milk.
* If you drink fresh milk , you will benefit a lot.

* إني أنصحك بأن تشرب حليباً طازجاً. إنك إذا شربت حليباً طازجاً, فإنك
سوف تستفيد كثيراً.

* If you don't do that, you will lose a lot.

* وإذا لم تفعل ذلك , فإنك سوف تخسر كثيراً.

* أما إذا أردت أن تنفّر الناس من أمرٍ , فمكنك أن تستخدم مثل هذه التراكيب:

* I **don't advise** you to drink wine.
* **It is dangerous to** drink it.
* **If you drink it , you will lose** a lot.
* **If you drink it , you will lose** your life .
* **If you drink it , you will suffer** a lot.

إن تشربه فإنك سوف تعاني كثيراً.

* حاول أن تقلد التراكيب السابقة عندما تريد أن تتحدث عن موضوع ما.

كل ما يجب أن تفعله هو أن تستبدل فعل بفعل أخر.

* في الجمل السابقة استخدمنا الشكل الأول للفعل عندما نريد الحديث عن حقائق في الوقت الحاضر.

2- The second verb-form الشكل الثاني للفعل

* We use this form when talking about past events

* نستخدم هذا الشكل عندما نتحدث عن أحداث وقعت في الماضي.
* I **played**   football yesterday.
* I **didn't play** tennis.
* We **went** swimming last Friday.
* We **didn't go** shopping last Sunday.

* حاول أن تركب جملاً مماثلةً باستخدام أفعال أخري مع مراعاة أن تذكر تأثير   ما قمت به عليك أو على الغير. خذ هذه الأمثلة وقلّدها.

* I **went** to the zoo with my family.
* I **rode** an elephant .   ركبت فيلاً .
* I **enjoyed** that a lot.   إني استمتعت بذلك كثيراً .
* That **impressed** me a lot.   إن ذلك أعجبني كثيراً .
* That **appealed to** me a lot.   إن ذلك راق لي كثيراً.
* I **found** a great pleasure in doing that.

إني وجدت متعة كبيرة في هذا العمل.

* Ali **did** something wrong. He **dropped** rubbish everywhere.

إن علياً قام بشيء خاطئ . إنه قام بإلقاء القمامة في كل مكان.

That **was** bad. I **didn't like** it.

That **scared** me a lot.   ذلك أمر أفزعني كثيراً.

That **depressed** me a lot.   ذلك أمر أحبطني كثيراً.

That **displeased** me a lot.   ذلك أمر غمني كثيراً.

That **saddened** me a lot .   ذلك أمر أحزنني كثيراً.

That **disgusted** me a lot.   ذلك

قــززني كـثـيراً .

* حاول أن تستفيد من هذه التعبيرات عندما تتحدث عن أمور حدثت في الماضي مع ذكر تأثيرها.

3- **The third verb- form** الشكل الثالث للفعل

* We usually use this form when talking about an event that happened in the past ,but still affects people and things at present .

* نستخدم هذا الشكل عادة للحديث عن حدث وقع في الماضي ولكن لا يزال هذا الحدث يؤثر على الأوضاع القائمة.

* We **have built** many roads.   * لقد بنينا الكثير من الطرق.

Thanks to بفضل these roads , we **have solved** many

   traffic problems.   * لقد تم حل الكثير مـن المشـاكل المروريـة. We

have reduced accidents.   * لقد قللنـا مـن الحـوادث . We **have**

made traffic easy.   لقد جعلنا حركة المـرور سـهلة. * Traffic jams **have**

disappeared   الاختناقات المروريـة قد اختفـت. *   Thanks to the new

shopping centre ,

   shopping **has become** a great pleasure.

* بفضل مركز التسوق الجديد , أصبح التسوق متعة كبيرة.

* I **have passed** with high marks,   لقد نجحت بدرجات عالية.

   but Ali **has got** bad marks.

نستخدم الفعل في الشكل الثالث للتعبير عن شيئ وقع في المـاضي و لا تـزال لـه علاقـة بالحاضر.

4-The fourth verb – form الشكل الرابع للفعل

* يستخدم هذا الشكل للحديث عن أمر أو أمور تحدث حا لياً كما يتضح من هذه الأمثلة.

* I **am reading** a book now.	* إني أقرأ كتاباً الآن. Ali

is watching TV at the moment.

* Mona **is feeding** her baby now.

* It **is raining** now.	* إن الـدنيا تمطر الآن.

We **are learning** English .

* They **are talking** about business.

* يستخدم الشكل الرابع أيضاً للحديث عن أمر كان يحـدث في لحظـة مـا مـن الماضي . أفحص الأمثلة التالية وتدّرب على تكوين جملٍ مماثلة.

* I **was helping** my mother at 5 o'clock .
* Ali **was washing** his car an hour ago.
* I **was reading** a book *when* you **phoned** .

كنت أقرأ كتاباً عندما اتصلت .

* هنا حدثان. أحدهما (قرأة الكتاب) كان يحدث قبل الأخر (الاتصال) إن قرأة الكتاب كانت مستمرة في الماضي ثم حدث الاتصال أثناء القرأة.

* Ali **went out** *when* عندما I **was studying** .
* They **came** *while* بينما we **were having** lunch.
* *While* I **was going** home , I **met** Hamad .

* نستفيد من هذه الجمل وأمثالها عندما نريد أن نروي أحداثاً وقعت في الماضي. بعضها حدث أثناء أحداث أخرى كانت تحدث قبلها.
* حاول أن تكون جمل مماثلة متبعاً نفس الطريقة.

15

How to carry out your writing task
كيفية القيام بتنفيذ عمل كتابي

First, you should know the topic : what you are writing about. It is necessary that you understand the thing that you are going to write about to ensure that you produce a successful piece of writing.

أولاً : عليك أن تعرف الموضوع الذي ستكتب عنه.

The next step is that you choose your topic sentence ,
the sentence that contains the main idea. You can choose one
of these sentences :   ثانياً : إختر جملة إفتتاحيه تعبر عن الفكرة الرئيسة

* فإذا كنت ترى الموضوع مهماً , فيمكنك أن تختار واحدة من هذه الجمل الافتتاحية.

* I want to write about the importance of ....
* I want to tell you about the importance of ....
* I would like to shed light on the importance of ....

* أود أن أسلط الضوء على أهمية ....

* أما إذا كان الموضوع فيه ضرر وخطورة , فيمكنك أن تختار واحدة من هذه الجمل

* I want to write about the danger of ....
* I want to tell you about the danger of ....
* I would like to shed light on the danger of ....

Third , use suitable adjectives to describe your topic .

ثالثاً : استخدم صفات مناسبة لوصف موضوع الكتابة.

* Food is **important**. Food is **useful** . Food is **necessary**.
* Nobody can deny that food is useful.

* لا أحد يستطيع أن ينكر بأن الغذاء مفيد.

* Smoking is **bad**. Smoking is **wrong**.

 Smoking is **dangerous**. Smoking is **harmful**. التدخـين ضـار

 Nobody can deny that smoking is bad for health.

* لا أحد يستطيع أن ينكر بأن التدخين ضار بالصحة.

Fourth, use suitable verbs relevant to your topic.

رابعـــاً: اســـتخدم أفعـــالاً مناســـبة لهـــا صـــلة بالموضـــوع .

* We **benefit** a lot from food.   إننا نستفيد كثيراً من الغذاء.

 We **need** food a lot because we **benefi**t a lot from it.

 We need books a lot because we benefit a lot from them.

 We benefit a lot from food , so we should eat it.

 We benefit a lot from books , so we should read them.

* **I advise you to** eat the right food .

* **It is necessary to** eat fresh food .

 If you eat good food , you will benefit a lot.

 If you eat good food , you will live well.

 If you do not eat good food , you will suffer a lot.

* إذا لم تتناول طعاماً جيداً , فإنك سوف تعاني كثيراً.

 If you do not eat good food , you will lose a lot.

 If you do not eat good food , you will **get ill**. تمرض

* أما إذا كان الموضوع سيئاً فإننا يمكننا أن نستخدم بعضاً من هذه الجمل.

* We **suffer** a lot from smoking.   إننا نعاني كثيراً من التدخين.

We **do not need** it because it is bad.

 We **suffer** a lot from **smoking** , so we should **fight it**.

* إننا نعاني كثيراً من التدخين ولهذا يجب أن نحاربه.

 We suffer a lot from silly TV **programmes** , so we
 should **avoid them**.

* إننا نعاني كثيراً من برامج التلفاز السخيفة , ولهذا يجب أن نتجنبها.

* I advise you to stop smoking .

  I advise you to avoid smoking.

* It is important to stop smoking.

  It is necessary to prevent منع smoking in public places.

* It is wrong to smoke .

  It is mad to smoke.

* If you smoke , you will suffer a lot.

  If you smoke , you will lose a lot.

  If you smoke , you will lose **lose your life** . تخسر حياتك

  If you smoke , you will <u>endanger</u> others . يعرّض للخطر

* It is right that we should fight this danger.

إليك بعض الجمل التي يمكنك أن تستفيد منها عند التحدث عن موضوع تراه جيداً.ويمكنك أن تطوّع هذه الجمل لكي تفيدك عند الحديث عن مواضيع أخرى.

* The advantages of (...........................) are certain .

  * إن مزايا .... مؤكدة .

* Nobody can deny the advantages of (the Internet , democracy ...).

  * لا أحد يستطيع أن ينكر مزايا ....

  *

(..) can improve our life a lot.

  * .... يمكن أن يحسّن حياتنا كثيراً.

* Thanks to (.......................) , we can develop ourselves a lot.

  * بفضل .... إننا نستطيع أن نطور أنفسنا كثيراً.

* Thanks to (.......) , (...........) has become a great pleasure.

  * بفضل .... , ... أصبح (أصبحت) متعة كبيرة .

* (..............) has made (...........) a great pleasure.

  * Thanks * .... قد جعل (جعلت) .... متعة كبيرة.

to (...........) , we can overcome many problems.

18

* بفضل .... إننا نستطيع أن نتغلب على مشاكل كثيرة.

* Thanks to (...........) , we have changed for the better.

* بفضل .... لقد تغيرنا إلى الأفضل.

* Thanks to (..........) , we will change a lot for the better.

* بفضل .... إننا سوف نتغير كثيراً إلى الأفضل.

* Thanks to (..........) , we can change our life for the better.

  =   =   =   , =   =   =   = country for the better.

  =   =   =   , =   =   =   = way of thinking.

↓

* طريقة   تفكيرنا

* Thanks to (........) , we have achieved a lot of things.

* بفضل .... , لقد أنجزنا الكثير من الأشياء.

* (...) is a great achievement that will change our life for the

  better. يعتبر إنجاز عظيم سوف يغير حياتنا إلى الأفضل. .... * * We are proud of

this great achievement.

* إننا فخورون بهذا الإنجاز العظيم .

* I assure you that this(these)(....) will benefit our people

  a lot.

* إني أؤكد لكم بأن هذا (هذه) .... سوف تفيد أهلنا كثيراً.

* Thanks to this achievement , life has become easy and

  comfortable.

* بفضل هذا الإنجاز , فإن الحياة قد أصبحت سهلة ومريحة.

* I think that (.........) will flourish a lot thanks to (.......) .

* إني أعتقد بأن ...... سوف يزدهر (تزدهر) كثيراً بفضل.....

* Nobody can ignore that (.......) will lead to stability and

  prosperity.

لا أحد يستطيع أن ينكر بأن .... سوف يؤدي إلى الاستقرار والرخاء .

* Since (.........) means prosperity , we should protect it.

* بما أن ...... يعني الرخاء , يجب علينا أن نحميه.

*(.............). means a lot to all people , so it is our duty to take care of it.

19

* .... يعني الشيء الكثير لكل الناس , ولهذا **من واجبنا أن نهتم به** (بها) .

* I advise you to use (......) well. If you do that , you will
  benefit a lot. But , if you **misuse** يسيئ إستخدام (it , them) ,
  you will lose a lot

* وفي الختام يمكنكم الاستعانة بإحدى هذه الجمل :

* We can say that (........) (is / are) useful , so we should
  (use / protect) (it / them) well.
* I hope that our people will protect this great achievement.
* I hope that our people will benefit from ....
* I hope that our people will use (this / these) ....
  to improve their lives.
* All in all , smoking is bad. We hope for a smoking- free
  country. We should fight to realize this noble goal.

* وخلاصة القول , إن التدخين سيئ . إننا نتطلع إلى بلد خال من التدخين.
ويجب علينا أن نناضل لكي نحقق هذا الهدف النبيل .

* In short , reading is useful , so we should read good books.
* It is true that we spend a lot of money on (........) , but the
  advantages are great.

* It is * * صحيح أننا ننفق الكثير من المال على (......) , ولكن المزايا عظيمة.
not wrong to use .... , but it is wrong to do that at the
  expense of our morals.

* ليس من الخطأ أن نستخدم ..... ولكن الخطأ أن نفعل ذلك على حساب أخلاقنا.

تعبيرات مفيدة Useful expressions

* إذا كنت ترى الموضوع سيئاً , فيمكنك إن تستخدم هذه الجمل بعد أن تعدّل فيها
بحيث تناسب الفكرة التي تتحدث عنها.
* Nobody can deny the disadvantages of (...............)

20

* * لا أحـد يستطيع أن ينكر مسـاوئ ....

Smoking hurts people a lot.

    Bad films **spoil** people a lot . * الأفلام السيئة تفسـد الناس كثيراً .

* (........) **endanger(s)** lives a lot, * يعـرّض الأرواح للخطـر . so it is

necessary to **fight** (it / them). ولهذا من الضروري محاربتها .

* (........) (is / are) a (big / serious خطيرة) problem , so we

should do something to **solve** it.

    * .... مشكلة كبيرة , ولهذا يجب أن نعمل شيئاً لحلها .

* If we solve it , we will **relieve** people. نخفف من معاناة

    If we solve it , we will **save** lives. ننقذ / الأرواح

* (.......) is a real danger , so we should do something to

  remove this danger.

    * .... خطر حقيقي , ولهذا يجب أننا أن نعمل شيئاً لإزالة هذا الخطر .

* It is unwise to **ignore** this danger .

    * ليس من الحكمة أن نتجاهل هذا الخطر .

* (..........) (have / has) **created** خلقت many problems.

* Nobody can deny that (........) (have / has) a bad effect

  on our young people , so we cannot **tolerate** (it / them).

* لا أحد يستطيع أن ينكر بأن ...... لها تأثير سئ على شبابنا , ولهذا فإننا لا نستطيع أن

نتساهل فيها .

* Everybody should **co-operate** يتعاون to **put an end to**

  this serious problem. يضع حداً لــ

    * كل شخص يجب أن يتعاون لكي يضع حداً لهذه المشكلة الخطيرة .

* (........) **means** a waste of time and money , so I advise

  people to do something else.

    * ......(يعني / تعني) مضيعة للوقت والمال , ولهذا فإنني أنصح الناس بأن

يفعلوا

شيئاً أخر .

وللخاتمة يمكنكم أن تختاروا واحدةً من هذه الجمل .

* We can say that …….. (is / are) dangerous , so we
  should do something to remove it.

* I hope that our people will **follow** يتبع my advice.

* I hope that our people will benefit from this information.

* I hope that this information will **appeal to** لـ تروق our people.

* I hope that our people will **act** يتصرف quickly to
  confront ليواجهوا this imminent danger. هذا الخطر الوشيك.

* I hope that this problem will **disappear** soon.

* أمل بأن هذه المشكلة سوف تختفي في الحال.

* I hope that people will act quickly to solve this serious
  problem .

* أمل بأن الناس سوف يتصرفون بسرعة لحل هذه المشكلة الخطيرة .

****

For مع / against ضد

* هناك مواضيع تتطلب أن توضح رأيك فيها . في هذه الحالة يمكنك أن تستفيد من هذا المثا
ل.

* **Write about this topic :**
  Tourists are coming in great numbers to our country.
  What do you think of that ?

** I want to tell you <u>my opinion of tourists coming</u>
  <u>to our country in great numbers.</u>   ↓

لاحظ أننا حذفنا are لنحصل على جملة اسمية.

I am for that because we benefit a lot from that .
Nobody can deny the advantages.

22

* **Write about this topic :**

The government has decided to raise ترفع bread prices.
What do you think of this decision? القرار

***I want to tell you my opinion of (the government)
raising bread prices.

I want to tell you my opinion of the decision to
raise bread prices.

* أريد أن أخبركم برأي في القرار برفع أسعار الخبز .

I am against that unfair decision because many people will suffer a lot
from that.

* إنني ضد ذلك القرار الظالم لأن كثيراً من الناس سوف يعانون كثيراً من ذلك .
* Nobody can deny the disadvantages of this unfair decision.

* لا أحد يستطيع أن ينكر مساوئ هذا القرار الجائر .
* ثم تقوم بذكر المزايا إذا كنت مؤيداً أو العيوب إذا كنت معارضاً.

* هناك حالات تستدعي الحديث فيها عن المزايا والعيوب .
هنا تتحدث عن المزايا في فقرة وعن العيوب في فقرة أخرى.
وأقترح بأن تختتم بعبارة شبيهة بهذه:
* We can say that ......(have / has)advantages and
disadvantages. We should **do our best** نبذل ما بوسعنا to
develop لكي نطور the advantages and reduce نقلل من the
disadvantages. I think that this is possible.
* It is good to travel (.......) to other countries , but you
should take care.
* It is good to use the Internet , but you should take care that
any **misuse** سوء استخدام of the Internet will bring **a disaster** كارثة.
* من الخير أن تستخدم الانترنت , ولكن يجب أن تأخذ الحذر أن أي سوء استخدام
للإنترنت سيجلب كارثة.
* It is good to have freedom , but we should take care that any
misuse of freedom can be disastrous .

* من الخير أن يكون لدينا حرية , ولكن يجب أن نأخذ الحذر من أن أي سوء استخدام للحرية يـمكن أن يكون كارثياً.

* It is good to (do , learn ....) , but that should not be at the expense of our (heritage تراث , culture ثقافة , traditions عادات , language , national interests مصالح وطنية) .

* من الخير أن (...........) , ولكن ذلك لا يجب أن يكون على حساب
(تراثنا , ... مصالحنا الوطني)   * I am for freedom of (choice الإختيار , opinion الرأي , expression التعبير) , but I am against any misuse of freedom.

** إنني مؤيـد لحريـة (....... , ... , ...) , ولكننـي ضـد أي سـوء اسـتخدام للحريـة.
Some TV programmes are **harmful** , others are **useful**.

We need useful programmes . We should **fight** to **realize** this
noble goal.

* بعض برامج التلفاز ضارة , والبعض الأخر مفيد . إننا نحتاج برامج مفيدة .   يجب
علينا أن نناضل لكي نحقق هذا الهدف النبيل.

موضوع الإنشاء الناجح The successful composition

A composition is successful if both the ideas and structures
are perfect. Some people are good at form الصياغة , but they do not have
ideas . Here is some advice that helps you produce ideas .

يكون الموضوع ناجحاً إذا كان المضمون (الأفكار) والصياغة سليمة.
ولكي يتحقق ذلك :

1- You should understand the topic ; you should know if
   it is good or bad for people.

1- عليك أن تـفـهم الموضوع الذي تريد أن تكتب عنه .

2- You should say how it affects people . Does it affect people
   positively بشكل إيجابي or badly ? Does it **hurt** or **benefit** people?
   How does it **affect** يؤثر في people?

2- عليك أن تذكر إلى أي حد يؤثر في الناس سلباً أو إيجاباً.

3- If you have **a relevant idea** فكرة مرتبطة بالموضوع , try to think of
   other ideas related to this idea. Use your idea to produce other
   ideas branching off it. Start with

the main idea . Then mention other ideas that result from the main idea.

3- فكِّر في أفكار أخرى تتفرع من الفكرة المتوفرة لديك. تأمل النص التالي:

An earthquake زلزال hit a town in the north of the country **causing a lot of damage . محدثاً / الكثير من الدمار** . It killed hundreds of people . The earthquake destroyed hundreds of homes , thus making thousands of people **homeless.**

الزلزال دمر مئات البيوت جاعلاًً بذلك آلاف الناس مشردين

These homeless people are suffering a lot ; they are suffering from cold البرد and hunger الجوع . We should do something to relieve لكي نخفف من معاناتهم them. We should send urgent aid. معونة عاجلة We can send tents خيام , food and medicine دواء . If we do that ,we will relieve them. If we don't act نتصرّف quickly , they will suffer more.

* نلاحظ أننا بدأنا بفكرة رئيسة تم تطرّقنا إلى أفكار متشعبة منها .وبهذه الطريقة نتغلب على مشكلة قلة الأفكار.

* Study this text to see how one main idea is used to **generate** لكي تولد other **relevant ones** أفكاراً أخرى مرتبطة بها.

If you go to Britain on holiday , you will find the people friendly , so I advise you to make many friends. I advise you to **mix with** people a lot . If you do that , you will benefit a lot . If you mix with people , you will **improve** your English. Once your English improves , you can **communicate** with people **with confidence**. This **communication** is useful **in the sense** that you **become able** to **take part in** any **dialogue** . The more you talk to others , the more you improve your **way of thinking.**

mix with يختلط مع / improve يحسّن, يتحسن / once وعندما
communicate with يتفاهم مع , يتصل مع
with confidence بثقة
communication الإتصال – التفاهم
in the sense that بمعنى
become able تصبح قادراً

take part in   يشارك في

dialogue   حوار

your way of thinking   طريقة تفكيرك

Composition 1 / The Summer holiday العطلة الصيفية

* Write about how you spent your last summer holiday.

     I am happy to write to you. I want to tell you about my last summer holiday. I went to Lebanon for my holiday. I had
a good time there . I did many things . When I **arrived** , I **booked** a hotel and **hired** a car. I drove to many places . I went to a park , where I **fed** ducks and **pigeons.** I enjoyed that a lot. I went to a zoo , where I saw many animals . I took some pictures of monkeys and **peacocks.** I went to a **museum,** where I saw old and new things. I went to the beach , where I spent a lot of time **lying on the sand** . That **amused** me a lot. Lebanon's mountains are wonderful , so I spent a lot of time climbing them.

     The Lebanese impressed me a lot. I enjoyed their delicious food . I found them friendly , polite and helpful , so I made many friends. I also enjoyed the fine weather.

     I feel happy because my holiday was **a success.**

arrived   وصلَ   /   booked   حجز فندقاً   / hired   استأجرَ
pigeons   الحمام   /   ducks   البط   / peacock   الطاووس
museum   المتحف   /   amused = impressed   أمتع- أسرني
The Lebanese   اللبنانيون   / a success   نجاح- ناجحة

* Complete these sentences in the same way :

1- I went to a zoo , where ------------------------------------- .
2- We went to a beach , where ------------------------------- .
3- They came to a place , where they ------------------------
    ---.
4- I went to a bookshop , where -------------------------------
5- Mona went to the supermarket , where ----------------------
    ----

Composition 2 / Camping التخييم
* Write about this topic : Why you like to go camping .

   I want to tell you why I like to go camping. I like camping because I benefit a lot from it. I learn many good things ; I learn how to **rely on** myself. I like camping because it **means** freedom and adventure. When I go camping , I feel free to do what I like. When I go camping, I meet new people and **exchange** ideas with them . This will improve my way of thinking. **Thanks to** camping , I travel to other countries, where I see a different way of life. That gives me a great sense of amusement . Thanks to camping , I have time to **practise** my hobbies.

   I **assure** you that camping is **a great pleasure**, so I advise young people to go camping . I am sure that they will enjoy it. It is useful to go camping , but we must **make sure** that we **benefit** from it . Camping is fun , but we should **take care** that we don't **misuse** it.

** Key words :

camping التخييم / rely on (1) يعتمد على / adventure (2) مغامرة
free حر / freedom الحرية / meet يلتقي بـ / exchange a
أفكار ideas (3) / يتبادل
great sense of amusement (4) إحساس كبير بالمتعة
practice (5) يمارس / hobby هواية / hobbies هوايات / assure (6)
يؤكد لـ / a great pleasure (7) متعة كبيرة
make sure يتأكد / take care يأخذ الحذر /
misuse يسيئ استخدام

----

* محاولة للنطق :   1- ري لاي / 2- أدڤن تشا (ر) / 3- أي دياز /
4-يوز منت / 5- براك تس / 6- أشو(ر) / 7- أقريت بليجا (ر) .

Composition 3 / Sports
* **Write about the importance of sports أهمية الرياضة**

   Say why sport is important .. what sports are popular
and what   sports you advise people to play.

   I want to tell you about the importance of sports.
Nobody can deny that sports is useful. People benefit a lot from sports.
Nobody can deny the advantages. First, some people practise sports to spend
their free time. Other people practise sports to get fit . **It is said that** يقال بأن the
sound mind is found in the sound body. This means that physical fitness leads to
mental fitness. Second , when you practise sports, you learn good things. You
learn how to be tolerant , helpful and decent. Real sportsmen have a sporting
spirit . Third , some people practise sports for fame and money. These people
play a game for money . There is nothing wrong with that because sports is
their means of living .

   Some sports are popular ; many people are playing sports like football ,
basketball , volleyball , running , skating

28

and rally-driving. These sports appeal to millions of people. Some people practise sports, others are fans of sportsmen.

Sports is useful, so I advise people to practise sports like swimming, jogging and camping. I am sure that sports is good for all people.

In short, it is good to practice sports, but you should take care that this does not cause you problems.

* Key words :

benefit يستفيد / useful مفيد / importance أهمية

deny ينكر / advantages مزايا / practise يمارس sound mind عقل

physical fitness (1) اللياقة البدنية / mental fitness (2) اللياقة العقلية tolerant (3) متسامح / sound body جسم سليم سليم

fame الشهرة / متسامح

sporting spirit روح رياضية / sportsmen الرياضيون

appeal to تروق لـ / means of living وسيلة للمعيشة

fans المشجعون / decent مهذب

nothing wrong with لا عيب في

----

* ملاحظة نطق : 1- فيزي كـا ل فت نس / 2- منتا ل فت نس

3- تولي رانت .

* Fill in the spaces with suitable words from the list:

1- Nobody can .... that sport is good for all.

2- We .... sport because we .... a lot from it.

3- If you practise sport, you will have a ....mind and a .... body.

4- Physical fitness leads to تؤدي إلى ....

5- Real sportsmen are .... , ... and helpful.

6- Some people practise sports for .... and money.

7- Sports is a .... of living for most sportsmen.

8- Some sports .... me, others do not.

9- There is nothing .... with playing a game for money.

10-You don't play any game, but you have a ....

11-Football .... are greater in number than others.

29

12- .... are people who either practise sport or
love it .

* Some people practise sports <u>to</u> spend their free time.

لكي وتعبّر عن الهدف من عمل ما ويأتي بعدها فعل شكل أول.

* Some people practise sport to get fit .

بعض الناس يمارسون الرياضة لكي يكتسبوا اللياقة .

* Some people practise sport <u>for</u> من أجل fame.

تعبّر عن الهدف أيضاً ويأتي بعدها اسم .

بعض الناس يمارسون الرياضة من أجل الشهرة .

Composition 4 / Safety at home .

*Write about the importance of safety at home السلامة في البيت

I want to tell you about safety at home. Safety is important because
we cannot live in danger . We need safety a lot. But how can we get it ?
It is easy to keep yourself safe from danger. We can get safety if we are
careful. We can get safety at home if mothers take care. Most accidents
happen at home because mothers are careless. Nobody can deny this fact.

It is easy to avoid accidents . If we follow some rules, we will
avoid accidents. Mothers should not let children play with matches.
Mothers should not allow children to play in the kitchen. The kitchen is
not a playground. It is wrong to put too many plugs into one socket.
Parents should watch their kids while playing in the garden. It is easy to
do these things .

These things do not cost a lot , but any mistake can cost you a lot. Don't be careless , or you will pay for it.

We can say that being careful means safety and being careless means danger. You have to choose , but you will have to pay for your choice. It is important to be careful because that reduces the possibility of having an accident.

** Key words :

let يدع- يسمح   القوانين-التعليمات rules / يتبع follow / يتجنب avoid
socket ساكت(كهرباء) / plug بلا ق / playground ملعب / يسمح لـ allow /
cost يكلّف / mistake غلطة / kids الأطفال / parents الوالدان
pay for يدفع الثمن / choose يختار / choice اختيار
reduce يقلل من / possibility إمكانية

* Fill in the spaces with words from the list:
1- We can .... accidents at home.
2- We should .... some rules .
3- It is wrong to .... kids play on their own.
4-It is wrong to .... kids to play with matches.

5-The kitchen is not a ....
6-If you make a .... , you will pay for it.
7-This big mistake will .... you a lot.
8-It is important to .... good films for our kids.
9 - We have freedom of ....
10- We are free to .... what we like.

* Language :
* It is wrong to let kids play alone.
↓
* يأتي بعدها اسم ثم فعل شكل أول بدون to .

* It is wrong allow kids to play in the kitchen.
↓
*يأتي بعدها اسم ثم فعل شكل أول مع to .
* We don't allow smoking . إننا لا نسمح بالتدخين

31

** Choose the right verb-form :

1 – I can't allow you (smoke – to smoke) here.

2- He doesn't (allow-let) me to travel **on my own**. بمفردي

3- He has allowed me (to use – use) his computer.

4- We don't (let – allow) walking here.

5- He always lets me (to sit – sit) here.

6- We are not allowed (leave – to leave) before the lesson ends.

7- Ali has a driving licence رخصة, so he is allowed

(drive- to drive) a car.

8- You can let Ali (doing – to do – do) this job.

9- We are (allow – allowed) to stay here.

10- It is wrong to let kids (swim – swimming) alone.

Composition 5 / Your Country .
** Write a composition about your country :

I want to tell you about my country . (Qatar) is an Arab Gulf country. It is a small country with a small population. (Doha) , the capital, is a modern town with superb buildings and green areas . Qatar is famous for oil and gas . Thanks to oil, life has changed a lot for the better. The people are friendly and hospitable. The people grow fruit and vegetables . Some people catch fish and build fishing boats.

Visitors can do a lot of things . They can watch horse and camel- racing. They can visit forts and the Oryx Farm in the North of the country. They can spend a good time on the sandy beaches in the South of the country. Qatar is also famous for its magnificent mosques and sports facilities. I am sure that a visitor to Qatar will have a good time. Qatar has a lot of interesting things that appeal to everybody.

I hope that this information is useful.

* Key words :

population السكان / superb فخم / green areas مساحات خضراء
famous for مشهور بـ / thanks to بفضل / hospitable مضياف
forts قلاع / oryx المها /sandy beaches شواطئ رملية/north شمال
south جنوب / facilities منشآت / appeal to تنال إعجاب - تروق لـ

* Fill in the spaces with words from the list :

1-Qatar is .... for oil and gas.
2-My country is famous for its .... mosques
   and .... beaches.
3- We have excellent sports ....
4-You can go to the Oryx Farm in the .... of the country.
5- have sand dunes كثبان رملية in the .... of the country.
6-Qatar has a lot of interesting places that .... to
all.

Composition 6 /Pen- friends أ.أصــدقــاء الــمراسـلة

* Write about this topic :
Many people have pen-friends in different countries.

I want to tell you my opinion of having a pen-friend. I am for having a pen-friend because we benefit a lot from pen-friends. Nobody can deny that we need pen-friends a lot. We cannot live alone ; we need somebody else to share us our ideas. Pen-friends learn from one another. They can exchange information and experiences. If you have a pen-friend , you will improve your writing skill. If you have a pen-friend , you will improve your English.

I have a pen-friend in England. I and Tom exchange letters. I enjoy reading Tom's letters because they are full of fun. I sometimes call him . I am happy because my English is improving.

In short it is interesting to have a pen-friend. If you have a pen-friend , you will learn many good things. If you don't have a pen-friend , you will lose a lot. I advise you to have a pen-friend lest your life should become boring . Don't miss the pleasure of having a pen-friend. It is good to have a friend , but you should take care that bad friends will spoil you.

* **Key words :**

opinion الرأي / ا / a pen-friend صديق المراسلة /

alone بمفرده / share يشارك- يشاطر / ideas أفكار

exchange يتبادل information معلومات /

improve يُحسّن-يتحسن / spoil يُفسد

experience (1) تجربة / writing skill مهارة الكتابة

full of مليئة بـ / fun الترويح – المرح – اللهو / call يتصل بـ

interesting ممتع- مشوق / boring ممل /

Don't miss لا تضيّ / pleasure (2) متعة

become تصبح / in short وخلاصة القول

....

ملاحظـة نـطـق : 1. إكس بير يانس / 2. بليجار

Composition 7 / Your School مـدرسـتـك
* **Write a composition about your school .**

I am happy to tell others about my school . I go to Doha School in the middle of my town. The building is modern and has the best facilities. It has excellent playgrounds , a first-class canteen and many green areas . There are 15 classes , a gym , a lab and a library .My school is doing an important job ; it teaches boys (girls) subjects like Arabic , English , Maths and Science. The teachers are kind, helpful and well-trained ; they are always ready to help every pupil. The pupils like the school , so they help mend broken chairs and desks. They also take care of the school . They keep it clean all the time. All the pupils are happy at this school because they feel that they are members of a loving

34

team. This school is using the Internet to enhance the pupil's learning skills.

I hope that my school will appeal to you. I advise friends to join it ; they will benefit a lot. They will find a real education centre. We hope for real education , so we should take care of our school to realize this noble goal.

Key words :

in the middle of في وسط   /   building المبنى   facilities منشأ ت   /   teach

علوم (سايانس) Science   /   رياضيات Maths   subjects مواد   /   يدّرس

well- trained مدربون جيداً   /   ready مستعد   /   mend يصلّح

develop يطور   /   broken مكسور   / take care of يعتني بـ   keep it

فريق متحاب a loving team   members أعضاء   /   يحافظ على نظافتها clean

/ appeal to تروق لـ   /   gym صالة ألعاب   a real education centre مركز

تعليمي حقيقي

excellent ممتاز/canteen مقصف   /   library مكتبة   lab مختبر

مهارات التعلم learning skills نحقق realize   /   نتطلع إلى hope for   /

* Fill in the spaces :

1-My school has excellent .... like a gym , a library
   and a lab.
                                                                2- My
school is .... an important job; it .... pupils
   many subjects.
3- Pupils learn subjects like Arabic , ... and
   ....
4- The teachers are kind , ... and ....
5- We need real education , so we should take care of our
   school to .... this goal.
6-You can .... you learning skills if you use the
   Internet.
7- My school is...................an important job ; it teaches
   useful ....

8- We are proud of our school because it is a real ....

....

9- I advise you to ....this school.

10- This school is a .... education centre.

Composition 8 / The knife

Write a paragraph describing the knife.

I want to tell you about the knife. Nobody can deny that the knife is useful . We need the knife a lot , so we should have one at home. It is important to have a knife. We need the knife to cut things. But the knife is sharp , so you should use it carefully. If you do not use it well , you will hurt yourself. We should also keep the knife away from children. It can cut them.

The knife is made of metal and plastic. It is used for cutting things. Thanks to the knife , we can cut things easily. The knife means a lot , but we should take care when we use it.

The knife is necessary , but we should use it well lest we should hurt ourselves. I hope that people will follow this advice.

* Key words :

cut (v) يقطع – يقص- يجرح / cut (n) جرح / hurt يؤذي
sharp حاد /take care يأخذ الحيطة /careful (adj.) (صفة) حذر
carefully بحذر / keep .... away from بعيداً عن ... يحتفظ بـ

* Fill in the spaces with suitable words:

1- The knife is ....,but we should use it ....

2- The knife is ...., so we should use it ....

3- If you use the knife badly , it will .... you .

4- I advise people to .... the knife well.

5- If you .... the knife badly , you will .... yourself.

6- He has got a .... Take him to hospital .

7- Thanks to the knife , we can cut things ....

8- Mothers should ....the knife away from their children .

9- I keep the knife away .... my kids for their safety.لسلامتهم

10-You should .... when you use the knife.

Composition 9 / A job you like.

* Write about a job you like to do .

I want to tell you about the job I like to do . Nobody can deny that the dentist is doing an important job ; he relieves people who have bad teeth. The dentist is necessary. It is important to have a dentist. If we don't have a dentist , we will suffer a lot. We have to see the dentist when we have a tooth-ache . He relieves us . The dentist also advises people to take care of their teeth. He tells people to brush their teeth after having food. He also tells people to avoid sweets because they spoil teeth.

However , the dentist scares children . Children don't like to visit the dentist because they experience a severe pain while the dentist is working with their teeth. But they have to visit the dentist because they cannot stand a painful tooth-ache.

So we can say that the dentist is doing a great job. We should respect him . We should teach our children that they must take care of their teeth if they don't like to visit the dentist.

* Key words :

dentist   طبيب أسنان / experience   يلاقي / relieve   يخفف من معاناة /
a tooth-ache   ألم أسنان   avoid   يتجنب / suffer   يعاني   /
brush   ينظف بالفرشاة / take care of بـ   يعتني / spoil   يفسد
pain   ألم/painful   مؤلم/ severe   حاد /scare   يرعب- يخيف   /
respect   يحترم / cannot stand   لا يستطيع تحمل   /

* Fill in the spaces with suitable words:

1- The dentist is doing an .... job. Nobody can deny this fact.

2- People with bad teeth must see the dentist ; he can ....
them.

3- If you suffer from a .... , you should ....the
dentist.

4- I have a .... tooth-ache , so I .... see my dentist.

5- It is .... to have a dentist

Composition 10 / Your favourite airline

طـــيـــرانـــك الـــمـــفـــضـــل

* Write a composition about this topic : Your favourite
air-line .

I would like to tell you about my favourite air-line.   I like Qatar Airways better than any other air-line. Qatar Airways is the best air-line in the world. Nobody can deny this fact . Thanks to Qatar Airways , flying has become easy and comfortable. Qatar Airways has made flying a great pleasure , so many people like to travel with them. Qatar Airways has attracted many people because they are flying to many places. Qatar Airways is flying to many countries in Asia, Africa and Europe. Another thing appeals to people; Qatar Airways has the best planes and the best pilots ; their planes are modern and their pilots are excellent.

All in all , Qatar Airways takes the lead in the field of air transport , so I advise everybody to fly with them. We are proud that Qatar Airways has done the economy of the country a great service.

* **Key words :**

travel السفر / flying جواً / air-line خط جوي / favourite مفضل

Africa أفريقيا / Asia أسيا / attracted جذب / يسافر

take / ممتاز excellent / أوروبا Europe / appeal to يروق لـ / the lead تحتل مركز الصدارة

field حقل – مجال / air transport النقل الجوي

economy do....a great service يؤدي خدمة كبيرة / اقتصاد

* **Read the above composition to fill in the spaces :**

1- Qatar Airways is the .... air-line in the ....

2- Qatar Airways is my .... airline ; I enjoy .... with them.

3- Thousands of people .... with Qatar Airways because they have made flying a great ....

4- Thanks to بفضل Qatar Airways , flying has become أصبح easy and ....

5- Qatar Airways is flying to .... in Asia,

.... and Europe.

6- Qatar Airways is attracting more and more ....
because they have modern ....and excellent
....

7- Qatar Airways is taking the .... in the field of
air transport .

8- We are proud of Qatar Airways because they have made
flying a ....

9- Qatar Airways has .... the economy of the
country a lot.

10- Thanks to Qatar Airways , flying has ....
Easy and ....

Composition 11 / Newspapers   الـصـحـف
Write a composition about newspapers .

I want to **shed light on** the importance of newspapers. Nobody can deny
that newspapers are useful. We benefit a lot from them, so we should read them.
The advantages of newspapers are great.   For one thing , newspapers provide
people with information about events that happen all over the
world. Thanks to newspapers , we get
up- to-date news of what is currently happening in every corner
of this globe , thus keeping us in touch with the outside

world. Newspapers also give people information about sports , art , health and business.

But what kind of newspapers do we need ? Of course , we need free newspapers that teach people freedom of opinion. Thanks to newspapers , we can see different opinions. Thanks to newspapers , people can express their ideas freely. This freedom of opinion is one of the major pillars of democracy . It is right to say that if we have freedom of opinion , we will have real democracy. Thanks to free newspapers , real democracy will flourish a lot.

In short , we can say that free newspapers are as important as oxygen , food and water. Accordingly , I advise people to fight for having free newspapers. A country with free newspapers can develop and flourish.

People need real , responsible journalism that provides
a good environment for democracy to flourish .

* Key words :

shed light on يسلط الضوء على   / advantages مزايا
importance أهمية   / for one thing أحد الأسباب up-to-date حديثة كا،
every corner   كا،
  / currently حالياً
ركن   / globe العالم   business المال
/ health الصحة
provide تزود - توفر   / freedom حرية
opinion الرأي   / express يعبر عن   ideas أفكار
/ freely بحـرية

the major pillars أركان أساسية   / express يعبر عن
real democracy ديمقراطية حقيقية   accordingly
يناضل من أجل fight for / وبناءً على ذلك   develop يتطور
/ flourish يزدهر   environment بيئة   /
responsible مسؤوله

* Read the above composition to complete these sentences :

1- I want to shed light on the .... of
    newspapers.
2- Nobody can .... that we benefit a lot from

41

newspapers.

3- Thanks to newspapers , we get .... news of
   what is happening in every ....of this
   ....

4- Newspapers are .... a good job ; they teach people
   .... of opinion .

5- Freedom of opinion is one of the .... of
   democracy.

6- It is easy for a country with .... to
   develop.

7- If we have real democracy , our country will ....

8-We are lucky to .... free newspapers in our country .

9-We cannot express our ideas .... We should
   .... freedom of expression. حرية التعبير

* **Re-order these words so as to form sentences :**

1- are / a / **Newspapers** / job / doing / good /
   ....

2- free / need / **We** / newspapers / because / want / we
   our / to / flourish / country /
   ....

Composition 12 / Young people .

Write about this topic: What do you think of young people? ما رأيك في
الشباب ؟

   I want to tell you what I think of young people. I think
young people are lazy and selfish. This is my opinion of young people.

   Young people are lazy. Nobody can deny this fact. Young people are
lazy for many reasons . First , they hate to work. They are unwilling to do
any kind of useful work. Second , they hate to help others ; they are
totally passive . They are good for nobody. That is unfair !

Young people are also selfish. They only care about themselves. They never care about others. They only think of their self-interests. They ignore other people . I don't expect this sort of young people to help others . They only want to have fun. This negative attitude is disappointing for others. However , there are some young people who are helpful and useful. I advise the unhelpful young people to change this shameful attitude. If they change , they will become an active part of their society. If they don't change , they will lose a lot . Other people will despise them.

In short , some young people are lazy and selfish . This attitude is unfair . They have to change it if they want others to respect them.

* Key words :

selfish أناني / for many reasons لأسباب كثيرة willing راغب / unwilling كاره / passive سلبي / بالكامل totally / self- / care about يهتم بـ / unfair ليس عادلاً / fair عادل، interests مصالح ذاتية / lose يخسر ignore يتجاهل / expect /يتوقع من this sort of هذا النوع من fun اللهو / attitude موقف- مخيب disappointing / however ومع ذلك / negative سلبي / مسلك لأمال

shameful مخزي / helpful متعاون / useful مفيد an active part of جزء فاعل من / society (1) مجتمع despise يمقت / respect يحترم

* Fill in the spaces with suitable words :

1- Young people are lazy; they are .... to work.

2- They are .... because they are good for nobody.

3- Some young people are .... ; they only care about themselves.

4- They ....other people. This attitude is shameful.

5- I expect you to .... this shameful attitude.

6- I expect you to become an active part of your ....

7- I advise you to change this bad attitude. If you do that , other people will ....you. If you don't change , people will .... you.

8- This negative attitude is .... for other people .

9- Some young people only think of their ....

10- Some young people are helpful and useful, others are .... and ....

* **Re-order these words so as to make sentences:**

1- people / selfish / because / others / **Some** / about / don't / care / young / are / they /

....

2- are / to do / young / **Some** / useful / any / unwilling / people / work /

....

3- this / have to / shameful / **They** / attitude / change /

....

4- become / society / an active part / should / of / **They** their /

....

Composition 13 / Islam and prayer .

* **Write a composition about this topic : " Islam and prayer."**

Islam is a religion , and the people who believe in this religion are called Muslims . Islam calls for the belief in the oneness of Allah (God). Muslims believe that Islam is the only answer to every problem facing people. Islam is the only way of life that makes people happy and comfortable all the time. Allah wants all people to believe in Islam.

If you don't believe in Islam , you will displease Allah. This means that Allah will punish people who refuse to believe in Islam.

The main pillar of Islam is prayer . Prayer is very important because it is the backbone of Islam. If you pray , you support Islam. If you don't pray , you destroy Islam. Muslims pray for Allah to show that they only worship Him. Muslims pray to be close to Allah. How do Muslims pray ? The Prophet of Islam asks his fans to pray in the same way he does it . Muslims pray five times a day. They have to wash before they pray. Muslims have to face Mecca when they pray. It is better for a Muslim to pray in the mosque . If you pray in   a group , you will benefit more.

We can say that Islam is Allah's religion ; if you believe in it, you will win. If you don't believe in it , you will lose . Muslims pray to please Allah . Allah wants Muslims to live according to Islam.

* Key words:

belief دعو إلى / call for / يؤمن بـ believe in / (1) religion دياته

the only answer الحل الوحيد / refuse يرفض / oneness وحدانية / الإيمان – الاعتقاد

way of life أسلوب حياة / الحل الوحيد

mean يعني / punish يعاقب / displease يغضب

backbone العمود الفقري / the main pillar الركن الرئيسي

destroy يدمر – يهدم / support (2) يساند- يناصر

worship يعبد / يُظهر – يُبرز – يوضح show

Prophet (3) نبي – رسول / لكي يتقرب من to be close to

to please لكي يرضي / fans أنصار

according to حسب – طبقاً لـ / in a group في جماعة

ملاحظة نـطـــق : 1- ريليجن / 2- سابورت / 3- برو فت .

* Fill in the spaces with suitable words :

1- Muslims are the people who الذين ....in Islam.

45

2-   Muslims believe in the .... of Allah.

3-   If you believe in Islam , you will ....Allah.

4-   Allah will .... people who don't believe in Islam.

5-   Muslims pray to .... Allah. If you don't pray , you will
     .... Allah.

6-   Prayer is the main .... of Islam. People who pray for Allah
     .... Islam. If you don't pray , you .... Islam.

7-   Islam is the only ....to every problem.

8-   Islam is a way of .... If Muslims follow it , they will be
     happy and comfortable. It they don't live according to Islam ,they will
     .... miserable (1) تعساء .

9-   It is better to.................... in a group. If you do that , you will ....
     more.

10- I advise you to pray . If you pray , you will .... You will win
     paradise (2) الجنة .

11-If you refuse to pray , you will .... If you
     don't pray ,you will ....Allah . If that happens ,
     you will certainly go to hell جهنم .

Composition 14 / Your country's achievements   منجزات بلدك

* **Write a composition about this topic :**
                " **The achievements of your country** ."
          " **The changes made in your country.**"

   I want to shed light on the achievements of my country. My country has
achieved a lot of things in many fields. Nobody can deny this fact. We can see big
changes everywhere. People

live in modern homes with running water and electricity. We have schools and colleges everywhere , where our children learn useful things. We are proud of the big number of the educated people. We have hospitals and health centres everywhere . These places provide free health services . Thanks to planes ,cars and buses , people can travel easily . Thanks to the satellite TV stations , people get to know more about other countries . We are lucky to have a huge network of wide roads , bridges and tunnels which make traffic easy and safe.

Thanks to these achievements , our life has become easier . Thanks to these achievements , we have changed for the better. These achievements mean a lot , so we should protect them.

Real changes have taken place in our country . We have more freedom of journalism . The number of free newspapers is increasing. Women no longer suffer from lack of job opportunities , so the number of working women has increased a lot. Women have become part of the political system ; some women are holding key positions in several ministries. We no longer have education problems ; you can see schools and colleges everywhere . These institutions provide real education for all people. People no longer suffer from power cuts or water shortages ; the government has set up more power and distillation stations .

In short , our country has achieved a lot , and we are proud of these achievements. I hope that we should have a sense of responsibility for these achievements.

* Key words :

achieve ينجز / achievement إنجاز / fields مجالاتchanges
تغيرات / electricity كهرباء / proud of فخور بـbig number عدد
كبير / educated متعلم / provide توفرfree health service خدمة
صحية مجانية / thanks to بفضل
satellite TV stations محطات التلفزة الفضائية / lucky محظوظnetwork
شبكة / bridge جسر / tunnel نفق traffic
حركة المرور / mean تعني / protect يحمي a sense of
responsibility إحساس بالمسؤولية

* Fill in the spaces with words from the above composition:

1- We have .... a lot of things in many fields.

2- We see big .... everywhere.

3- People live in modern houses with .... water and ....

4- Thanks to schools and colleges , we have a big ....of .... people. This is a great ....

5- People can .... easily thanks to planes and cars.

6- Hospitals .... free health service for everybody .

7- We are lucky to have .... roads which make .... easy.

8- We have .... TV stations that provide people with information about other ....

9- These achievements .... a lot , so we should ....them .

10- We have changed for the .... thanks to these achievements.

Composition 15 / An interesting experience تجربة ممتعة

* Write a composition about " An exciting , interesting experience .

One day , I went on a hunting trip with some friends. The weather was a little cloudy . While I was driving my Land Cruiser , I saw a small bird in the sky. I stopped and let my falcon chase it. The bird tried to escape , but the falcon could strike it with its strong wings . The bird fell down to the ground followed by the falcon .

I drove fast to the place where the bird fell, but unluckily my car got stuck in the sand. That displeased me a lot. I got off the car to see what happened. My friends appeased me saying that they could solve the problem. We began to clear the sand away from the wheels. I put some pieces of flat wood in front of the wheels and drove slowly until I got out of the sand. It was a tiresome job, but the view of the falcon carrying the prey refreshed all of us.

* Key words :

hunting trip رحلة صيد / cloudy مغيم / chase يلاحق / escape يطارد - يهرب

أجنحة wings / يضرب strike / يهرب escape

fall down يسقط / ground الأرض / followed by يتبعه- يلاحقه

fell down سقط / unluckily لسوء الحظ / sand غرزت got stuck الرمل

الرمل / displeased أغضب / appeased هدّأ clear away

هذبا / wheels العجلا / view منظر tiresome متعب /

prey الفريسة / refreshed أنعش falcon صقر

* Fill in the spaces with suitable words :

1- Last Friday , we .... a hunting trip in the desert.
2- I saw a bird in the sky and let my falcon .... it.
3- The bird tried to .... , but the falcon struck it with its strong ....
4- The bird .... to the ground .... by the falcon.
5- I drove to the .... , where the bird fell .
6- Unluckily , my car .... in the sand .

7- We began to .... the sand away from the ....

8- The job was tiresome , but the .... of the falcon carrying the .... refreshed all of us.

9- While I was driving , I saw a bird in the ....

10- I looked worried because my car got .... in the sand.

Composition 16 / A rally you watched.

* Write a report describing a rally you watched .

Let me tell you about a rally I watched last week. The rally took place in Dubai . About fifty racing cars took part in the competition. The competitors came from different countries. What impressed me most was the fact that young rally-drivers were racing against old champions . I was surprised because a young competitor beat all the other competitors , thus winning a Gold Medal. I could not believe it. Nobody expected that result.

The rally was a hard one. The competitors faced many problems. The most remarkable one was the weather ; it was terribly bad. The heavy rain turned the roads into rivers. Many cars got stuck in the mud . Other cars skidded and overturned. Some drivers got hurt and had to go out. The losers complained that they lost the race because of the bad weather conditions. Anyway , the young winner boasted saying that he could beat not only bad weather , but also old champions . The crowd cheered the young winner.

* Key words :

took place حـدثَ		took part شارك	
believe يصدّق		competition (1) المنافسة	
competitor (2) المتنافس – المتسابق	impressed أسعدني		race
against يتسابق ضد		champion (3) بطل	

51

surprised (4)	فوجئت	beat	يـهزم – هـزم
expect	يتوقع	result (5)	النتيجة
The heavy rain	المطر الغزير	The most remarkable one	أبرزها
turned ... into	أحالَ .. إلى	got stuck	غرّزت
skid	يتزحلق	overturn	ينقلب
got hurt	أصيب بأذى	complain	يشتكي
loser	الخاسر	weather conditions	الأحوال الجوية
anyway	وعلى أية حال	winner	الفائـز
boasted (6)	فاخـرَ	crowd (7)	الجـمهـور
cheered (8)	هـتفوا		

* ملاحظـة للنطـق : 1   كم بـيـتيشن / 2- كم بـيتيتـور   /   3   تشام بـيون

/   4 – سيـر بـرايـزد /   5-   ريـزالت / 6- بوسـتـد / 7- كـرا ود / 8-
تـشيـرد

Composition 17 / Why people travel .

* Write a composition about this topic: "Why people travel

لماذا يسافر الناس ؟ .

I want to shed light on why people travel to other places. Nobody can deny that travelling is useful ; people benefit a lot from it. Nobody can ignore the advantages. If you travel , you will benefit a lot. First , if you travel , you will see new places and new people. You will get to know a lot about other people. Second , thanks to travelling , you can make a lot of friends. When you meet new people , you have a chance to improve your English. Third , it is necessary for one to travel ; if you travel , you will change the routine of your life. When you travel , you will enjoy yourself . Fourth , many people travel for education and business . Some people study abroad , so they have to travel. Businessmen travel a lot , thus boosting trade relations with other countries.

In short , people travel for different reasons. We can say that travelling is a great pleasure. It is good for you to travel , but you should take care that you avoid whatever may cause you trouble. It is not wrong to travel , but the important thing is that you benefit from it.

* Key words :

deny يتجاهل ignore / يستفيد benefit / مفيد useful
improve / فرصة chance / المزايا advantages / ينكر
يحسّن / study يدرس / routine روتين - رتيب / enjoy yourself
تمتّع نفسك / education التعليم business (1) التجارة والمال
/ businessmen رجال أعمال abroad بالخارج / boost
cause you يحسّن - يزيد
trade relations (2) يسبب لك متاعب trouble
for take care يأخذ الحذر / علاقات تجاريه)
different reasons / whatever أي شيئ / لأسباب مختلفة
a great pleasure (3) متعة كبيرة boost يدعم - يعزز - يشجع /

ملاحظة نطق : 1- بيزنيس / 2- تريد ريليشنز / أقريت بليجار

53

* **Fill in the spaces with suitable words :**

1- Nobody can .... that travelling is .... ; people .... a lot from it .

2- If you travel , you will .... a lot.

3- People travel to other .... for different ....

4-Some people travel to ....in foreign universities. جامعات أجنبية

5- Businessmen travel for ...., so they boost trade .... with other countries.

6- Some people travel to change the .... of their life.

7- Thanks to travelling, you can .... a lot of friends , thus improving your English.

8- Nobody can deny the .... of travelling.

9 - If you travel , you will .... yourself.

* **Language** لغــة :

1- Businessmen travel a lot ,so ولهذا they boost trade relations with other countries.

* إن رجال الأعمال يسافرون كثيراً ولهذا فإنهم يعـززون العلاقات التجارية مع البلدان الأخرى

* نستخدم/ so /لربط جملتين – الجملة الثانية ناتجة عن الجملة الأولى.

* يمكن أن نستبدل أداة الربط بأخرى مثل thus :

2- Businessmen travel a lot , thus boosting trade relations with other countries.

* نلاحظ بعد أداة الربط استخدمنا فعلاً في الشكل الرابع بعد أن تم حذف الفاعل .

54

Composition 18 / Weddings   الأفـراح

* Write a composition about this topic :
"Weddings in the Gulf and Britain . "

حفلات العرس في الخليج وبريطانيا

I would like to shed light on weddings in the Gulf and Britain. You will see big differences. First, weddings cost a lot of money in the Gulf , but they cost much less money in Britain. Second , the Gulf people do not allow men to mix with women in the wedding party , but in Britain men can mix with women. Third , the Gulf people , unlike the British people , invite many people to the wedding party and offer the guests a big meal . Fourth , the Gulf people can have the wedding party in the open air , whereas the British people usually have the wedding party in a hotel. Finally , in the Gulf friends help the bridegroom with the costs of the wedding , but in Britain people give the married couple simple presents.

In brief , we can say that weddings are different from one place to another , but there is a common thing ; all people have a wedding party to show pleasure and share the married couple joy.

* Key words :

different مختلف / difference فرق – اختلاف / cost كلفة-يكلّف allow

يسمح لـ / mix with يختلط مع / unlike بخلاف invite يدعو

/ offer يقدّم / guest (1) الضيف

in the open air في الهواء الطلق / bride (2) العروس

bridegroom العريس / the married couple (5) الزوجين

simple presents هدايا بسيطة / in brief (3) وباختصار

a common thing شيْ مشترك / show يُظهر

share يشارك / pleasure (4) الـسـرور - الفرحة

joy الفرحة

----

* ملاحظة للنطق : 1- قيـست / 2- بـرايـد / 3- إن بـريـف /
4- بـليـجار / 5- ما ريد كا بل

55

* **Fill in the spaces with suitable words from the above list :**

1- Weddings in the Gulf are ....from those in Britain. Nobody can deny that there are big ....

2- Weddings .... a lot of money in the Gulf , but in Britain they .... much .... money.

3- The Gulf people , ... the people in Britain, do not ....men to mix with women.

4- The Gulf people .... a big number of people to the wedding and offer them a big ....

5- The Gulf people like to have the wedding party in the ....
....

6- The Gulf people usually help the bridegroom with the .... of the party.

7- All weddings have a .... ; people want to show .... and share the married couple their ....
.

* **Language   لغـة :**

1- Ali , <u>like</u> Nasser مثله مثل , likes يحب music .
 Both Ali and Nasser like music. إن كلاً من علي وناصر يحب الموسيقى.
2- Hamad , <u>unlike</u> Ali , likes sport .
 إن حمداً , خلافاً لـ علي , يحب الرياضة.
* الكلمتان اللتان تحتهما خط يتم استخدامها للتعبير عن التشابه أو الاختلاف بين طرفين .

* **Rewrite the following sentences using " like and unlike " :**

1- I and Nasser speak English alike .
 ....

2- Nasser and Jassim hate lazy people in the same way.

 ....

Composition 19 / Rally- driving سـباق الـسيارات

* **Write a composition about this topic :**
    " What you think of rally – driving. "

I want to tell you my opinion of rally-driving . I think that rally-driving is dangerous. Nobody can ignore the danger of rally-driving . First , the rally-drivers drive too fast on tough roads. This might cause terrible accidents . The rally-drivers endanger their lives because speed means death . Second, I am against rally-driving because the racing cars are too expensive ; they cost too much money. We could use this money to feed hungry people or to build houses for homeless people. Third , rally-driving is a waste of time . Rally-driving is bad because rally-drivers waste time .... time that they could spend doing useful things . Why not spend time for the good of all people ? Isn't it mad to spend time taking risks ?

In short , rally- driving is bad , so we should stop this dangerous sport and give people something useful and interesting .

* **Key word :**

ignore يتجاهل / (1) tough عنيف
cause (2) يسبب – يتسبب في / endanger يعرّض للخطر
lives أرواح / speed السرعة
against ضد / expensive (3) غالية
feed يطعم / hungry جوعان
homeless مشردين / a waste of time مضيعة للوقت
waste يضيّع – يبدد / spend ينفق – يقضي
for the good of لمنفعة – لصالح / take risks يركب المجازف

----

* ملاحظة للنطق: 1- تَف   /   2- كوز   /   3- اكس بنسف

58

Composition 20 / The importance of food   أهــمــية الـغـذاء

I would like to write about the importance of food. People need food simply because they need **energy**. People need food to **grow**. It is impossible for any **living creature** to **stay alive** without food.

People need different kinds of food. Some foods give people protein which is necessary for **growth**. Meat, fish and eggs are rich in protein. Carbohydrates like honey, rice, potatoes and bread provide people with energy. Fresh vegetables and fruit are rich in minerals and vitamins that **protect** people from disease.

It is important to know what kind of food we should eat. People should eat **nutritious** foods. You need to have a **balanced diet**; it is wrong to focus on one kind of food. Your meal should be a **mixture** of different foods. **It is worth saying that** good nutrition leads to good health. If you eat well, you will live better. If you are well-fed, you will become healthy. Healthy people enjoy life better than unhealthy ones. **Contrarily**, if you have unhealthy food, your health will **get worse**. Badly-fed people **suffer from ill-health.**

The **state** of your health also **depends on** the **amount** of food you eat. We should eat what we need. If you eat too much, you will get fat. It is bad to be **overweight** because **obesity puts stress on the heart**. You **exhaust** your heart by being too **obese**.

In short, food is necessary for people, but we should **make sure** that we have the right food. Good health is everybody's goal. We should use balanced food to **realize** this noble goal.

* **Key words** كلمات أساسية :

energy الطاقة / growth (قرووث) النمو / grow ينمو
stay alive يبقي حياً / living creature (كري تشا) مخلوق حي protect
nutritious (نيو تري) يحمي / isease (دي زيز) المرض
nutrition التغذية / (شاس) مغذٍ

mixture (مكس تشا) مزيج / balanced diet طعام متوازن

obesity (اوبي ستي) البدانة / It is worth saying that ويجدر القول بأن

lead to تؤدي إلى / contrarily (راري لي) وعلى العكس كونت

get worse تسوء – تتدهور / suffer from يعاني من

ill-health اعتلال الصحة / stat حالة / depend on تتوقف على

amount (أماونت) كمية / exhaust (إقزوست) تجهد- تتعب

overweight = obese بدين / make sure يتأكد

realize (ريا لايز) يحقق / put stress on تضع عبئاً على

* Fill in the spaces with suitable words :

1- Food is important because it gives people ………………..

2- Vegetables are rich in minerals and vitmines that
   …………………… people from disease.

3- We should eat …………………. food. This kind of food
   leads to يؤدي إلى good health.

4- We should eat the right ……………… of food. It is wrong
   to eat too much . If you eat too much , you will become
   ……………………… .

5- It is important to know that ……………… puts stress on the
   heart.

6- Good health is everybody's ……………….. . We should have
   ………………. food to ……………… this goal.

60

Composition 21 / The value of Reading قيمة القراءة
Write a composition about this topic :

" Reading is your key to knowledge."

It is very important to be able to read the language you are learning. Reading is a skill that you can develop through practice. What do we mean by reading ? Of course , we mean both loud and silent reading.

Why do we read ? We read for information. We have to understand what we read. The more you read , the more ideas you get. But to be a good reader , you should be familiar with the basics of the English grammar. Your knowledge of grammar helps you understand what you   read . Once you understand what you read , your reading skill improves. We read because we get most of our knowledge through reading.

But we face difficulties while reading. How can we overcome this problem? We should try to guess the meaning of a word from context .. from the place it takes in the sentence. Other words in the same sentence help you guess the meaning of a difficult word. Another important thing, it is wrong to insist on knowing the meaning of every word. You needn't do that. It is possible to get the meaning without knowing the meaning of every word. I advise you to learn as many verbs as possible. A verb is the main component of a sentence. Once you know the meaning of the verb , it becomes easy to guess the meanings of the other words in the sentence.

We read for information . If one is good at reading , he can improve his writing skill easily. The language skills are closely related. We should know that without reading , it is impossible to develop the other language skills.

● **Key words :**

meaning / develop ينمي / skill مهارة / قادر able
المعنى / (1) through practice عن طريق الممارسة
familiar صامتة silent / جهرية (2) loud
improve grammar القواعد / على دراية بـ (3) with
تتحسن (4) knowledge
المعرفة / (5) difficulty صعوبة (6) difficulties صعوبات
/ overcome نتغلب على (7) guess نخمن /
context (8) السياق insist on (9) يصر على
/ verb الفعل sentence الجملة مهارة skill /
على (10) closely related
صلة وثيقة / without بدون

ملاحظـة نـطـق : 1- ثـرو بـراك تـس / 2- لاؤ د / 3- فـا ميـل يـار وذ
4- نـا لـدج / 5- ديـفي كالتـي / 6- د يـفي كالتيـز
7- قـس / 8- كُـن تكـسـت / 9- إن سيـسـت /
10- كـلوز لي .

62

Composition 22 / Prevention الوقاية

* Write a composition about this topic :

" Prevention is better than cure . " الوقاية خير من العلاج

Nobody can deny that prevention is better than cure . Prevention is easier than cure. It is easy to prevent a disease , but it is difficult to cure it. It is easy to prevent a problem , but it is difficult to solve it. Prevention does not cost you a lot , but cure does. Prevention does not take time , but cure does. We can prevent a disease if we fight flies. Fighting flies is much easier than curing a disease they carry . Preparing for an exam is less painful than failure. You study to avoid failing an exam. Failure has very bad consequences ; it might lead to more serious problems . Being careful keeps you safe from danger , and that does not cost too much. Being careless , on the other hand , endangers your life . You do not pay too much for being careful , but you may have to pay too much for being careless. We immunize our children to keep them safe. That does not cause much trouble. That is a form of prevention. But if you do not immunize your children , they will probably catch a disease that will cause too much trouble for everybody .

All in all, prevention is much less troublesome than cure. The wise person always opts for prevention because it saves time and trouble. It is good to take care , but it is wrong to be careless.

* Key words :

prevent يمنع – يتقي	/ prevention الوقاية	المنع – الوقاية
cure (v , n) علاج-يعالج	/ solve يحل	cost يكلّف
/ fight يكافح- يحارب		flies الذباب
/ disease (1) المرض	less أقل	/ pass an
exam ينجح في امتحان	painful مؤلم	/ fail an
exam يرسب في امتحان	lead to يؤدي إلى	/
bad consequences (2) عواقب وخيمة		
serious (3) خطير		

keep you safe from يجعلك في مأمن من / pay for يدفع ثمناً

immunize يطعّم / cause trouble (4) يسبب عناءً

catch a disease يصاب بمرض / avoid يتجنب

troublesome متعب – مسبب للعناء / wise person الشخص العاقل

opt for يختار / prepare for يستعد لـ save trouble يوفر

carry تحمل – تنقل / العناء

----

* ملاحظة نطق: (1) ديزيز / (2) كن سيك وانسيز / (3) سيرياص / (4) كـوز ترابـل

*Fill in the spaces with suitable words :

1- Nobody can .... that prevention is better than ....

2- It is easy to ....a disease ,but it is difficult to .... it.

3- .... is easier than cure .

4- Prevention , unlike cure , does not .... time.

5- Flies .... disease , so we should .... them. Fighting flies is much .... than curing disease.

6- Preparing for an exam is painful , but it is much .... painful than failure . Failure has very ....consequences.

7- Being careful is an example of مثال على .... We take care because we want to .... problems.

8- We immunize our .... because we want to keep them ....disease. Immunizing children is a form of شكلاً من ....

9- Prevention does not .... you a lot. You don't have to pay too much for that .

10- Prevention saves time and ....

* Language لغـة :

1- You study hard to **avoid** **failing** an exam.

↓

* يأتي بعدها اسم على هيئة فعل شكل رابع .

2- **Being careful** keeps you safe from danger.

أن تكون حذراً (اسم) ┗

64

Composition 23 / Smoking   الــتـدخيــن

* Write a composition about this topic : " The dangers of smoking. "

I want to shed light on the dangers of smoking . Nobody can deny that smoking is bad for health. We suffer a lot from smoking . Smoking is dangerous because it can destroy health. If you smoke , you will lose your life. If you smoke , you will spoil your teeth. If you smoke , you will destroy your lungs. If you smoke , your children will smoke too.

Smoking is a serious problem , so we should do something to solve it. It is possible to solve this problem. First ,people should stop smoking . If you stop smoking , you will save your life. You should stop smoking to relieve others. Second , we should prevent smoking in public places. People should not smoke in shops , hospitals or on planes. Third , we should prevent students and teachers from smoking inside the school building. Fourth , the Ministry of Education should not give a job to a smoker.

All in all , smoking means slow suicide , so I advise smokers to give it up if they want to survive the danger of smoking. I advise non-smokers not to allow smoking everywhere. We can say that smokers are brainless people because they know that smoking is a killer.

* Key words :

destroy يدمر / spoil يُفسد / health الصحة
lungs (1) الرئتان / serious problem مشكلة خطيرة
solve يحل / save ينقذ / relieve (2) يخفف من معاناة
prevent يمنع / fight يحارب / in public places في الأماكن العامة mean
يعني / survive (3) ينجو من
Ministry of Education وزارة التعليم / suicide (4) انتحار
brainless مجنون / a killer قاتل

----

* ملاحظة نطق : 1- لنـقـز / 2- ريليـﭫ / 3- سرﭬايـﭫ / 4- سوسايد

65

* **Fill in the spaces with suitable words :**

1- Smoking is ……………, so it is wrong to ……….. . If you
smoke, you will …………………….. your health.

2- If you smoke, you will …………………………. your teeth.

3- Smoking can damage your …………. . If this happens, you
will have a breathing problem. مشكلة في التنفس

4- You do not breathe well because you ……………… .

5- Smoking is ………………… ; if you smoke, you kill yourself.

6- Smoking is a ………….. problem, but we can ………….. it.

7- We should …………………………. smoking in public places.

8- If you give up smoking, you will ……………… its danger.

9- It is wrong for ……………...... to smoke inside the school
building.

10- Non- smokers should not ………………… smokers to
smoke everywhere.

* **Re-order these words to make sentences :**

1- have / problem/ a / **You** / breathing / smoke / because / you/
……………………………………………………...............

2- so / is / give it up / **Smoking** / should / bad / you
……………………………………………………..............

3- in / should / places / smoking / public / prevent / **We** /
……………………………………………………...............

4- means / so / death / why not / **Smoking** / up / it / give /
……………………………………………………...............

5- you / will / smoke / If / you / your / destroy / health
………………………………………………………………

66

Composition 24 / The traffic policeman شـرطي الـمـرور

* **Write a composition about the traffic policeman.**

I would like to tell you about the traffic policeman. Nobody can deny that we need the traffic policeman a lot. He is doing a very important job ; we need him to control traffic . Thanks to the traffic police , traffic becomes easy and safe, so we don't see traffic jams or serious car accidents. We need the traffic police to make sure that everybody follows the traffic rules. Thanks to the traffic police , people follow rules lest they should pay a fine. If you break rules , the police will fine you . Therefore , it is wrong to break rules. It is right to follow rules. If we follow rules , accidents will disappear , and our roads will become safe.

We can say that the traffic police are doing us a great service ,so we should respect them . If we respect them , they can do their job well. People need the traffic police to control traffic . Thanks to the traffic police , people don't have traffic problems.

* **Key words :**

do a job يقوم بعملٍ	/	control ينظّم – يراقب
thanks to بفضل	/	traffic حركة المرور
become يصبح	/	traffic jams اختناقات
make sure (1) يضمن – يكفل	/	follow يتبع
fine يغرّم – غرامة	/ traffic rules (2) قوانين المرور	pay a fine
يدفع غرامة	/ lest خوفاً من أن	
break يخرق	/ our roads طرقنا	
disappear (3) يختفي	/ respect يحترم	
do us a great *service* (4) يؤدي لنا خدمة عظيمة		
serious (5) خـطيـرة		

----

* ملاحظة نــطق : 1- ميك شور / 2- ترافك رولز/ 3- دس أبير / 4- سيرڤيس / -5 سـيـريـاس

67

1-We follow rules **lest** we **should** pay a fine.

* إننا نتبع القوانين خوفاً من أن ندفع غرامة.
* للتعبير عن خوفنا من شئ ما فإننا نستخدم هذا التركيب.

2- They do us a good service.   إنهم يؤدون لنا خدمة عظيمة .

* Complete these sentences :

1- We study hard إننا ندرس بجد lest ....

2- I am driving slowly lest I ....

3- I am doing this job carefully lest ....

4- Teachers are doing a very ....job ; they

    educate يعلّم our children .

5- The soldiers الجنود protect the country , so we should

    ....

* Fill in the spaces with suitable words :

1- We need the traffic police to .... traffic.

2- Nobody can .... that the traffic police are

    .... a good job.

3- We should have traffic police to .... that people

    follow the traffic ....

4- I always write slowly to .... that I don't make

    a mistake خطأً .

5- Thanks to the traffic police , we don't see any ....

6- Thanks to the traffic police , traffic becomes يصبح ....

7- If we drive carefully بحذر , accidents will ....

8- We are happy because our roads have ....

    safe.

Composition 25 / A fire حـريـق

* **Write a composition describing a fire you saw .**

Last Monday morning , I was walking on my way to school when I saw a house on fire. I ran as fast as I could to see what happened. When I arrived , the fire was blazing out of control. But I rushed into the house to save the people trapped inside the house. It was difficult to see anything because of the thick smoke . As I was moving inside the house , I found a child crying . I pulled the child to the outside of the house . I had some slight burns , but I did not care . The firemen arrived and began to fight the fire . In less than half an hour , the firemen could control the fire , thus preventing it from spreading to the near-by houses. The firemen did a good job . Thanks to them , nobody was killed and the fire was put off in no time . I was proud of our firemen because they were ready for any emergency job.

I felt happy because I did a good job; I saved a child . I will never forget this daring rescue operation .

* **Key words :**

on my way to في طريقي إلى / on fire يحترق / blaze تشتعل out of control خارج نطاق السيطرة / thick smoke الدخان الكثيف / trapped محاصر / save ينقذ / rush يندفع / cry يبكي / hear يسمع / move يتحرك / pull يسحب
slight burns (1) حروق بسيطة / care يكترث
control يسيطر على / prevent يمنع
spread to يمتد إلى / the near-by houses البيوت المجاورة
thanks to them بفضلهم / put off a fire يطفئ حريقاً
in no time بسرعة / nobody was killed لم يقتل أحد
proud of فخور بـ / ready for مستعد لـ
emergency job (2) عمل طارئ / forget ينسى
daring جرئ - شجاع / rescue (3) إنقاذ
operation عملية

69

* **Language** لـغة :

1- I am **on my way to** school.   . أنا في طريقي إلى المدرسة

2- He was **on his way to** school. .إنه كان في طريقه إلى المدرسة

3- These boys are so bad ; they are out of control.   إن هؤلاء الأولاد سـيئون

.إنهم خارج نطاق السيطرة . (لا يمكن السيطرة عليهم.)

4- The firemen controlled the fire , thus preventing it from

spreading to other houses.   * سيطر رجال الإطفاء على الحريق , وهـم بـذلك

منعوها من الامتداد إلى بيوت أخرى.

5- I **prevent** you **from doing** that.

He has prevented me from **going out** at night.

. لقد منعني من الخروج ليلاً *

6- I am **proud** of my sons .   إني فخـور *

7- I am **ready for** the race.   .إني مستعد للسباق *

* **Fill in the spaces with suitable words :**

1- I saw a house .... fire. The fire was ....out ....

control.

2-Some people were .... inside the house ; we had to

do something to ....them. In fact , we made a

.... rescue operation.

3- We should .... people from smoking in this place. 4- We are

ready .... the exam.

5- We are proud .... our country.

6- I saw Hamad .... my way to the bank.

7- The firemen put .... the fire **in no time** بسرعة

8- I pulled the child .... the outside .... the house.

9-The fire did not .... to the near-by houses.

10- I had some .... burns , but I did not ....

Composition 26 / TV programmes

* Write a composition about this topic :
" TV programmes --- advantages and disadvantages."

I would like to tell you about the advantages and disadvantages of TV programmes. Nobody can deny the impact of TV programmes on people.

The advantages are great. Some programmes are useful ; they are interesting and instructive. If you watch good programmes , you will benefit a lot. Some programmes are amusing ; they provide fun for the viewer. Others are instructive ; they provide the viewer with useful information . Some TV programmes are useful because we learn useful things from them. These programmes amuse and teach people. TV programmes are not only a means of instruction , but also a means of entertainment. People need programmes that can entertain and teach them good things. People want to see useful programmes because they want to learn useful things.

But some TV programmes are bad and dangerous because they are full of shameful scenes. People do not need this kind of programmes because these programmes spoil young people . Bad programmes have a bad impact on children and young people. They teach bad things. Some programmes are full of violence and sex scenes . This is shameful ; we cannot accept that. It is wrong to show bad programmes. It is the duty of parents to make sure that their kids watch only good programmes. I am not against showing violence on TV , but I am against showing too much of it. Violence is part of our daily life. We cannot ignore that .

All in all , TV programmes have advantages and disadvantages .Some are useful . Others are bad. We should see good ones so as to learn good things. We should avoid showing bad programmes lest we should lose our kids. It is not wrong to see TV programmes , but it is wrong to see silly ones

* Key words :

advantages مزايا / disadvantages مساوئ / impact تأثير useful مفيد /

interesting ممتع / amusing ممتع /

instructive مثقّف – منوّر للعقل / provide توفر

fun اللهو – المرح / information معلومات / viewer (1)

يسلي – يرفه عن entertain / amuse يسلي / المشاهد

الترويج – التسلية entertainment

a means of instruction وسيلة تثقيف / shameful مخزي – مخجل scenes (2) مشاهد

young (3) people الشباب / accept (5) يقبل sex الجنس / violence (4) العنف / spoil تُفسد /

make sure / parents الأباء / duty واجب duty بـ

يتأكد من

avoid يتجنب / lest خوفاً من / kids أبناء

against ضد / part of جزء من

daily life الحياة اليومية / ignore يتجاهل / teach يعلّم

* Fill in the spaces with suitable words :

1- Nobody can deny the ………. of TV programmes on people.

2-TV programmes have ……………….. and …………………

3-Some are interesting ; they provide ………. for the ………..

4-Some are ……………….; they can teach people …………. things.

5-TV programmes can ………….. and ……………….. people.

6-TV programmes are a means of …………….......................... .

7-TV programmes are a ………………….… of entertainment.

8-Some programmes are full of ………….scenes . They show

   too much violence and too much ………….. . The shameless

   scenes ………….our kids.

9- I am ……………….… showing too much violence on TV.

10- I am against ……………………….. sex scenes on TV .

11- Parents should ……………….... that their kids watch good

    programmes.

12-It is your duty to make sure that your …………….…see good

    programmes.

13- If you allow your children to see bad programmes, you will

    …………............   them .

72

Composition 27 / Leisure (spare) time وقـت الفـراغ
* Write a composition about the importance of leisure.

I want to shed light on the importance of leisure. Leisure is free time. It is important to have free time. We need leisure time a lot. Nobody can deny the advantages of leisure time. If you have leisure time , you will get more energy. It is wrong to go on working without a break . If you go on working , you will get bored. This will have a negative impact on your productivity. This will diminish your concentration , thus paving the way for mistakes to take place. That is the reason why good companies get their staff to be off duty for some time . Leisure means high productivity. People need a change of air .

It is important to have leisure time , but the way you spend it is more important. It is necessary to spend your leisure doing useful things. You can spend it reading books and watching useful programmes. You can spend your leisure travelling to other countries or helping others solve their own problems.

In short , people need leisure to break the routine of life , but we should make the most of it. Leisure time is useful , but we should take care that it does not cause us problems.

* Key words :
leisure (1) وقت الفـراغ / deny ينكـر / advantages مزايـا energy طاقـة / go on يستمر / get bored يصاب بالملل / without a break دون توقف / impact تأثير productivity (2 الإنتاجية) / concentration (3) التركيـز / diminish يقلل – ينقص- يتنـاقص / pave the way for يمهد السبيل لـ mistakes أخطاء / take place تقع / get .... to تحمل- تجبر / reason (4) السبب -تحدث

73

break تغيير الأجواء change of air / يتوقف عن العمل be off duty

يكسر / make the most of من يستفيد أقصى فائدة

----

* ملاحظة نطق : 1- ليجر / 2- برودك تيڤيتي / 3- كن سنت ريشن / 4- ريزن /

* **Fill in the spaces with suitable words :**

1- Nobody can deny the .... of leisure.

2- It is important to ....free time.

3- It is wrong to go on .... without a break.

4- If you go on working , you will get ....

5- People need leisure to .... the routine of life.

6- If you ....working , your concentration will ....

7- If you go on working , your productivity will ....

8- People need a .... of air.

9- When you lose your concentration , ... will take place.

10- Loss of concentration فقدان التركيز paves the .... for mistakes.

* **Re-order these words to make sentences :**

1- important / is / leisure / have / **It** / to /

....

2- is / more / spend / leisure / your / is / you / way / **What** / important / the /

....

3- advise / reading / **I** / you / to / your leisure / books / spend /

....

4- should / others / help / problems / **We** / their / solve /

....

5-   should / **We** / to make / try / our leisure / the most of /

....

Composition 28 / Germs   الـجـراثـيـم

* **Write a composition about this topic : "** Germs are
  dangerous."

I want to tell you about the danger of germs. Nobody can deny that germs
are harmful. People suffer a lot from germs because they cause disease .   Germs are
very small living things that cannot be seen. They are so small that we have to use
a microscope to see them. .Germs are harmful , so we should fight them. Germs live in
dirty places. Flies carry germs , so we should kill them. We can use certain insecticides
for this purpose.

Germs are a big problem , so we should do something to solve it. We can
solve this problem if we do certain things. We can keep our kitchens and bathrooms
clean. We can boil our drinking water to kill the germs. We should cover our food to
prevent flies from touching it. It is important to immunize children lest they should
catch disease.

All in all , germs and flies are ruthless enemies ,so we should get rid of them
at any cost.

* **Key words :**

germs جراثيم   /   harmful ضارة   / (1) suffer يعاني
in dirty places في الأماكن القذرة / carry تحمل – تنقل
solve نحل   / (2) certain بعض – معينة
insecticide (3) مبيد حشرية / boil نغلي
certain things أشياء معينة   /   keep .... clean نحافظ على نظافة
drinking water مياه الشرب / (4) touch يلامس   / immunize نطعّم   /
lest خوفاً / (5) ruthless لا يرحم / (6) enemy عدو / enemies أعداء
/ get rid of يتخلص من at any cost بأي ثمن for this purpose لهذا الغرض /
living things أشياء حيـة

----

* ملاحظـة نطـق : 1- سَـفر / 2- سـيتن / 3- انسـكتي سـايد / 4- تاتـش /5- روثلـس /6- إنيمـي

75

Composition 29 / A typical day يــوم نـمــوذجي

* Write a composition about a typical day of yours.

I want to tell you about a typical day in my daily life. My day starts at 5:30 when I wake up. I wash and pray. As soon as I finish , I have breakfast. I always have bread , cheese , honey and fresh milk . Then I change my clothes and drive to school . At school , I study from 7:30am to 1:30pm . I learn different subjects ..... subjects like Arabic , English , Maths and History. I like my teachers a lot because they work hard to give us good education.

I get home at about 2:00pm. I have lunch with my family . After that, I usually lie in bed for about an hour before I start to do my homework . I usually finish at 7:00pm. In the evening , I visit a friend or go out for a walk along the Corniche. I enjoy that a lot. I get home to sit with my family. We always talk about family matters . When it is 10:00pm , I go to bed.

This is my lifestyle , and I can say that it makes my life easy and comfortable. I advise everybody to have a lifestyle of their own so that they can lead care- free lives.

* Key words :

typical day (1) يوم نموذجي / wake up يستيقظ
honey (2) عسل / change يبدّل
subject (3) مادة دراسية / get home يصل إلى البيت
have lunch with يتناول طعام الغداء مع /
education (4) تعليم / lie in bed يرقد في الفراش   a walk
مشوار مشي / family matters مسائل عائلية
lifestyle (5) اسلوب حياتي
lead a care- free life يعيش حياة خالية من الهموم

....

* ملاحظة نطق : 1- تيبي كال / 2- هـا نـي / 3- سَب جِكت /
4- إديـو كيـشن / لايف ستـأيـل

76

Composition 30 / Pet- hates المكدرات

● **Write a paragraph about your pet-hates.**

Nobody can deny that everybody has pet-hates. I , like other people, have my own pet-hates . Pet-hates are things that annoy you a lot , but you can do nothing about them . I suffer a lot from these pet-hates. I hate certain things . Take noise for example . I hate noise . It makes me nervous . I cannot stand people who shout . I hate people who drive noisily . That gives me a headache. Another thing , I cannot stand people who talk too much. These people talk in detail about things that you do not need to know. These people bore you to death before they stop talking. I hate people who smoke everywhere . These people smoke in placcs where smoking is not allowed. I get angry when I see a man smoking in a lift. These rude people annoy me more than anything else. I hate these unpleasant things , but I have to live with them simply because I cannot escape from them.

In short , pet-hates are ugly things . I urge everybody to do something to relieve others . It is not nice for you to do things that cause others trouble. If everybody cares a bit about others , the problem will disappear. It is not wrong to do what you like , but it is shameful that your actions offend others.

* Key words :

pet- hates   مكروهات -منغصات / annoy   تضايق
care a bit يهتم قليلاً بـ / suffer from   يعاني من   hate   يكره
certain(1) things أشياء معينة /
take ……. for example خذ على سبيل المثال
make me nervous (2) تـنـرفـزنـي   cannot
stand لا يمكنني أن أتحمل
a headache (3) صداع / in detail بالتفصيل
bore you to death يقتلوك بالملل- يمللك حتى الموت

disappear (4) تختفي / allowed مسموح به
rude (5) وقح / unpleasant (6) منفر
live with يقبل بها على مضض / escape (7) يهرب
urge (8) يحث   relieve يخفف من معاناة
shameful (9) مـخزي – مـخجـل   actions (10) أفعال
offend تـسـيئ إلى
....

* ملاحظة نطـق : 1- أ سـيـر تن / 2- نيـر قـاص / 3- أهيد إك /
4- دس أبـيـر / 5- رود / 6- أن بـلـيـزا أ نـت / 7- إس كيب /
8- إيرج / 9- شيـم فل / 10- أكشـنـز

* Fill in the spaces with suitable words :

1- I have my own ………………………….. .
2- Pet- hates are ugly things , but we can do nothing about them.
3- I hate people who ……………… too much noise.
4- I ……………….. people who smoke ……………………. .
5- It is not nice to ……………… others trouble

78

Composition 31 / Two friends of yours.

* Write a composition comparing two friends of yours.

Nasser and Ali are friends of mine . They are different in the sense that they are opposites. They are different in many ways. Nasser gets up early , but Ali gets up late. Nasser is careful , so he rarely makes a mistake. Ali , on the other hand, is careless , so he always makes mistakes. Nasser is hard-working , so he gets good marks at school. Ali is lazy , so he gets bad marks. Nasser has lots of friends , whereas Ali is self- centred . Ali hates making friends. Nasser likes music and sport while Ali likes travelling and reading.

Nasser and Ali are different , but they love one another. They think that one is free to choose his own way of life. Nasser and Ali are different , but they respect one another. They say that their differences do not spoil their friendship.

* Key words :

compare يقارن	different مختلف /
in the sense بمعنى	opposites (1) أضاد /
in many ways في مجالات كثيرة	
rarely نادراً	make a mistake يرتكب خطأً /
on the other hand من الجانب الأخر	hard-working مجدّ /
marks درجات – علامات	while = whereas في حين أن /
self- centred منطوي على نفسه	travel يسافر /
travelling السفر	free حر /
choose (2) يختار	way of life أسلوب في الحياة /
respect يحترم – احترام	different مختلف /
differences (3) اختلافات – فروقات	spoil يفسد /
friendship (4) الصداقة	one المـرء/ الشخص /

79

Composition 32 / The computer   الــحـا ســوب

● Write a composition about the computer .

Nobody can deny that the computer is a great achievement . People benefit a lot from it . The advantages are great. For one thing , the computer means a lot to people ; it means speed , thus saving time and trouble. The computer gives people easy access to the world of information . In fact , the computer has made information accessible ; people can reach a lot of information in a second . Another thing , the computer means accuracy ; it does not make mistakes. The computer is   a reliable source of information. Apart from that , the computer can work for long hours without getting tired , so it can replace a big number of working people. Lastly ,   the computer has put an end to the monopoly of information , thus making information available for all people .

The computer is doing people a good service . People are using it widely. Banks , companies and factories are using it to improve their performance .   I advise people to use it well if they want to make the most of this amazing invention. But the computer cannot replace the human brain , so we cannot rely totally on it. If we rely totally on it , we will spoil our brains. We have to dismiss the wrong idea that the computer can do everything for us.

In short , the computer is a useful invention , but it cannot solve all our problems.

* Key words :

achievement إنجاز / advantages مزايا / easy access مدخلاً سهلاً
great عظيم / world of information عالم المعلومات   totally كلياً /
accessible (1) سهل الوصول إليها   reach يصل إلى / speed السرعة
accuracy (2) الدقة   get tired يتعب / save time يوفر الوقت
save trouble (3) يوفر الجهد   unlike بخلاف /

without بدون / factory مصنع / أخطاء mistakes

factories مصانع / يؤدي خدمة عظيمة do a good service

solve يحل / companies شركات / company شركة

spoil يفسد كلياً totally / rely on يعتمد على / أداء performance (4)

dismiss يطرد – يرفض / يحل محل replace بشري human / الدماغ brain

monopoly (5) احتكار / يضع حداً لـ put an end to متوفر available

....

ملاحظة نطق : ١- أكسسي بَل / ٢- أكيو رَسي / ٣- سيق ترابل / ٤- بار فور مانس / ٥- منو بولي

* **Language** لغـــة :

1 The computer means speed , **thus saving time** .

* إن الحاسب يعني السرعة وهو بذلك يوفر الوقت .

2- Ali worked hard all his life , **thus making a big fortune.**

* إن علياً عملَ بجدٍ طيلة حياته وهو بهذا كون ثروة كبيرة .

* نلاحظ حدوث عملٍ ما نتج عنة حدث أخر ، وللتعبير عن النتيجة فإننا نستخدم **Thus** .

* **Complete these sentences in the same way :**

1- It was raining hard , thus ....

2- He pushed the door strongly , thus ....

3- They have built new roads , thus ....

4- We have introduced أدخلنا the computer , thus.............

....

5- The teacher is using simple language لغة بسيطة , thus

....

* The **world** of information عالم المعلومات

  The **monopoly** of information احتكار المعلومات

  A **source** of information مصدر للمعلومات

نلاحظ من الأمثلة أن هناك اسمان:عالم ، المعلومات ، وهـما مضاف ومضاف إليه.

وفي الإنجليزية لابد من وضع of بين المضاف والمضاف إليه .

* **Supply the missing words :**

1- The top .... the mountain قمة الجبل is covered with snow .

2- English is the language لغة .... computing.

3- Nobody can deny the advantages ....the computer.

4- All people share the joy فرحة ....the Eid.

5- I like this writer for the simplicity .... his language.

6- I **appreciate a lot** أقدّر كثيراً the accuracy .... your information.

* **Re-order these words to make sentences :**

1- the/performance/improved/ **Thanks to** /have/ computer/their/ banks

   ....

2- wrong / to / totally / rely / is / on / computer / **It** / the /

   ....

3- this / dismiss / **We** / idea / have to / wrong /

   ....

4- means / **The** / to / computer / people / a lot / all /

   ....

5- useful / a / computer / invention / is / **The** / , so / use / should / it / well / we /

   ....

6- saves / and / compuer / **The** / trouble / time.

   ....

7- misuse / will / **To** / the computer / spoil / everything.

   ....

Composition 33 / The importance of English

أهـميـة اللـغـة الإنـجليـزيـــة

* Write a composition about the importance of English .

      I want to tell you about the importance of English. Nobody can deny that we need English a lot. We benefit a lot from English , so we should learn it. We should know this important language. If we know English , we will benefit a lot. If we know English , we will understand other people better. If we don't know English , we will suffer a lot. If we don't know English , we will lose a lot.

      English is necessary in many fields . English is the language of trade ; businessmen use it widely. English is the language of tourism ; tourists need it a lot . English is the language of air transport ; pilots use English a lot. Doctors and sportsmen are using English a lot.

      English is a world language , so I advise people to learn it. It will benefit them a lot. It is easy to learn this language. You can join an English - teaching centre , where you can learn this language. You should practise the language a lot . You should also mix with native speakers of English . If you do that , you will learn this language easily.

      In short , English has become necessary because millions of people are using it . We need English so that we can communicate with others. We need English to have access to the world of the Internet. I hope that people will follow my advice.

* **Key words :**

important مهم / importance أهمية / deny ينكر
benefit from يستفيد من / know يعرف suffer from يعاني من
understand يفهم / necessary ضروري fields حقول - مجالات
language (1) لغة / trade التجارة
businessmen (2) رجال أعمال / tourism (3) السياحة

* ملاحظة نطـــق : ١- لانق وج / ٢- بزنس من / ٣- تورزم

tourist   سائح / air transport النقل الجوي
pilot (4)   الطيار / sportsmen الرياضيون / follow يتبع
a world language لغة عالمية   / advise (5) ينصح
have access to لدينا منفذاً إلى   / advice (6) نصيحة   communicate (7)
native speaker (8) الناطق الأصلي   /   يتفاهم

....

٤- بايلوت / ٥- أدفايز /   ٦- أدفايس /٧- كم يوني كيت /   ٨- نيـتـث
سبيـكا(ر)

* **Fill in the spaces with suitable words :**

1- Nobody candeny that we .... English a lot.
2- It is necessary to .... English . If you ....it , you will
.... a lot.
3- If you do not know English , you will .... a lot.
4- English is necessary in many ....
5- English is the .... of trade ; businessmen .... it
a lot.

* **Re-order these words to make sentences :**

1- has/ world / become / **English** / language / a /
.... 2- learn /
everybody / I / to / English / advise /
.... 3- using /
English / **Doctors** / widely / and / are /
businessmen
.... 4- know /
English / you / you / If / a lot / benefit / will /
.... 5- wrong /
at the expense of على حساب / is / It / Arabic / to
learn English/
.... 6- need / **We** /
communicate / others / English / to / with /
....

6- gives / to / the Internet / English / one / the world /
access

....

Composition 34 / Life in the Gulf and in Britain.

* **Write a**   الـحيـاة فـي الـخـلـيـج وبـريـطانيـا

composition comparing life in the Gulf and life in Britain.

I would like to compare life in the Gulf and life in Britain. It is important to know about life here and there. You will see many differences. First , cars drive on the right in the Gulf , but cars drive on the left in Britain. Second , shops open at 8:00 in the Gulf , but shops open at 9:30 in Britain. Third , the weather is too hot and humid in the Gulf, but the weather is cold in Britain. Fourth , the Gulf people are using air- conditioners for cooling the air, whereas people in Britain have central heating in their houses.

But you will find some common things. Both peoples love peace and freedom. Both love sports and travelling. Both are friendly and tolerant.

In short , life in the Gulf is different from life in Britain and this is natural because everybody has their own way of life . I hope that you will find this information useful.

* **Key words :**

compare يقارن بين / different مختلف / whereas في حين أن / difference فرق

اختلاف – / weather الجو / humid (1) رَطب   air- conditioner مكّيف

للهواء / central heating تدفئة مركزية

common things أشياء مشتركة / both peoples كلا الشعبين people – الناس

peace (2) السلام   الشعب /

freedom الحرية / travelling السفر

friendly ودود / tolerant (3) متسامح

natural (4) طبيعي   / everybody كل شخص

way of life أسلوب حياة

....

* ملاحظة نطق   ١- هيومد / ٢- بيس / ٣- تولي رنت / ٤- ناتشرال /

- Some people are tolerant .   بعض الناس متسامحون

- I like people who have a high sense of responsibility .

* أحب الناس الذين لديهم إحساس عال من المسؤولية .

* هنا كلمة people   اسم جمع .

* The Arab people is famous for hospitality.

الشعب العربي مشهور بكرم الضيافة .

The world's peoples are against war.

إن شعوب العالم ضد الحرب .

* هنا كلمة people   تعني "شعب" وهي مفرد .

* Life in the Gulf is **different from** life in Britain.

My car is different from yours.

Your house is different from mine.

* I want to compare life in the Gulf and life in Britain.

I want to compare life in the Gulf   to (with) life in Britain.

* **Fill in the spaces with suitable words :**

1- I want to .... life in the Gulf with that in Britain.

2- Life in the Gulf is .... from life in Britain in
many ways.

3- It is important to .... about life in Britain if you
want to stay there.

4- Cars drive .... the right in the Gulf , but cars drive
....   in Britain .

5- We have common things ; both of us love .... and
....

6-Everybody has their own .... of life . This is
....

7- Some people .... against this way of doing
things.

8- You are different ....your brother in many
   ways.

Composition 35 / A letter from a British pen-friend.

رسالة من صديق- مراسلة

*Imagine that you are English .Write a letter to a pen-friend
coming from the Gulf to study in Britain.

Dear Hamad ,

   I am happy to write to you. I am happy that you are coming to
Britain to study English. It is important to know about life here. You will see
many differences. First , cars drive on the left , so you must take care. Second ,
the weather is cold, so I advise you to get warm clothes with you. Third , the
education system is different ;   the students do not need to memorize
information. Boys and girls sit together in the same halls. Finally, here people eat
pork and drink wine. I know that Muslims neither eat pork nor drink wine .

   However , you will find the people friendly and open- minded , so
you can make friends easily. I advise you to do that. If you mix with many
people , you will improve your English. The people here respect freedom of
opinion and refuse to interfere in others' way of life.

   Life is different from life in the Gulf. It is important that you adapt
to it . If you fail to do that , you will suffer a lot. I am sure that you can adapt to
life here.

   I have this chance to welcome you to my country hoping that you
will benefit from my information .

                                                        Yours ,

                                                           Jim

* Key words :

take care   يأخذ الحذر / warm clothes ملابس دافئة
education التعليم   / system (1) نظام /
memorize (2) يحفظ غيباً /   pork   لحم خنزير
wine (3) الخمر   / open- minded متفتح الذهن
mix with يختلط مع   / improve يحسّن
respect   يحترم   / refuse (4) يرفض

freedom of opinion حرية الرأي / interfere in (5) يتدخل في
one's way of life طريقة حياة الشخص / adapt to (6) يتكيف مع

fail يفشل / suffer يعاني / others الآخرون
have the chance (7) يغتنم الفرصة
welome يرحب بـ / welcomed رحب بـ
....

* ملاحظة نطق : ١- سستم / ٢- ميمو رايز / ٣- واي ن / ٤- ريف يوز / ٥- إنتر فير /
٦- أدابت تو / ٧- هاڤ ذا تشا نص

* **Fill in the spaces with suitable words :**

1- I advise you to .... warm clothes because the .... is too cold.

2- The education .... is different ; the students do not need to .... information.

3- Muslims neither eat ....nor drink ....

4- The people are .... ; they .... freedom of opinion.

5- I advise you to .... with many people . If you do that , you will .... your English a lot.

6- It is important to .... to the way of life here. If you .... to do that , you will suffer a lot.

7- It is .... to know about life here.

8- It is bad to ....in others'private lives . الحياة الخاصة للآخرين.

* **Re-order these words to make sentences :**

1- find / friendly / will / people / **You** / the / nice / and /
....

2- to / is / many / easy / friends /in / make /country / **It** / this
....

3- useful / friends / to / is / **It** / many / have /

88

....

4- of / respect / opinion / **We** / freedom /

....

Composition 36 / Your problems with English.

مـــشـــكـــلا تـــك مـــع الـــلـــغـــة الإنـــجـــلـــيـــزيـــة

*Write a letter to a friend telling him about your problems
with English and asking him for advice.

Dear Jim,

I am happy to write to you . I am writing to tell you about my problems with English. I expect you to give me some advice.

I am learning English , but I am facing some problems. First , I have problems with grammar and spelling. I don't know how to make the sentence , so I cannot write anything . Second , I do not dare to speak to others because I fear that I may make a mistake. Third , I have reading problems because some English words have more than one meaning. Fourth , I do not have a reasonable amount of vocabulary because I cannot pronounce many words . I want you to show me how to learn vocabulary. Some people speak too fast , so I have difficulty in following them.

I suffer a lot from these problems which make me unable to learn this language well. I have many problems with English , but I am still willing to learn this important language. So I beg you to advise me what to do.

I hope that you will show me how to solve my problems with English .

Yours ,

Ali Nasser

* Key words :

face – facing يواجه / grammar القواعـد / spelling التهجـي
sentence جملة / dare يجرؤ / fear يخاف – يخشى
make a mistake يرتكب غلطـة / others الآخـرين
meaning معنى / reasonable (1) معقول
amount (2) كم - كمية / vocabulary (3) مفردات

show يري - يرشد / difficulty (4) صعوبة / suffer يعاني

unable غير قادر / still لا أزال / willing راغب

beg يرجو - يتوسل / solve يحل / pronounce (5) ينطق

words كلمات / expect (6) يتوقع من / follow يفهم

....

* ملاحظة نطق:١- ريزانابل / ٢- أماوت / ٣- ڤوكاب يولاري / ٤- ديفي كلتي
٥- بروناونس / ٦- إكس بيكت

* **Language** لغــة :

1- I have problems **with** English. لدي مشاكل في اللغة الإنجليزية

I have problems with grammar.

He has problems with his neighbours. لديه مشاكل مع جيرانه. 2- I have

difficulty(in) learning English. لدي صعوبة في تعلم الإنجليزية

* **Fill in the spaces with suitable words :**

1- I have some .... with English grammar. Can

you help me .... them ?

2- Ali has a problem .... Nasser . We should ....

something to **bring both to terms.** لكي نوفق بينهما

3- If you want to learn a language , you can start with

....

4- You have made many .... mistakes ; you cannot

spell easy words. If you want to improve your ....,

you should practise تتدرب a lot.

5- You should know how to make the ....**It is not**

enough to learn words. لا يكفي أن تحفظ كلمات

6- It is difficult to learn a word if you don't know how to

....it.

7- We should learn how to .... the word in a

sentence. Everybody should know how to .... the

90

sentence.

8- I ....not speak to others in English. I may make a
....

Composition 37 /   A car accident حادث سيارة
* Write a composition describing a car accident .

Last Sunday morning , the weather was a bit misty and rainy. I was
driving home when a man overtook me . He was driving too fast. At that
moment ,   a child was crossing the road. The mad driver did not see the
child because of the bad weather. When the driver caught sight of the child ,
he braked to avoid him. But it was too late . The driver hit the child knocking
him down . That frightened me a lot. I stopped and ran to save the child .
Other people hurried to the place . I called the ambulance , but the child died
on the spot. The traffic police soon arrived and began to investigate the
horrible accident .

This accident shows that it is necessary to do something to protect
innocent people from road hogs. I suggest that we should punish road hogs .
If we do that , we will reduce accidents . Car accidents happen because people
drive carelessly. It is important that we should do something to avoid car
accidents.

* Key words :

mist   ضباب   / misty   به ضباب / rain   مطر
rainy   ممطر   / overtook تجاوز / overtake يتجاوز
carelessly بإهمال   / catch sight of يلمح - يرى
caught sight of (9) رأى - لمح / braked فرمل / avoid يتجنبknock down)
1) أرضاً يطرح /   frighten (2) يرعب
hurry (3)   / hurried أسرع / يسرع show   تُظهـر
scene (4)   مكان الحادث   / on the spot في مكان الحادث
investigate يحقق في   / horrible   مرعب – مخيف
protect يحمي   / innocent (5) برئ
road hogs مجانين السرعة / suggest (6) يقترح
punish (8)   يعاقب   / reduce (7) يقلل من

91

* ملاحظة نطق : ١- نوك داون / ٢- فراي تن / ٣- هـري / ٤- سين /
٥- إني سا نت / ٦ ساجيست / ٧- رد يوس / ٨- با نيـش /
٩- كـوت سا يـت أُڠ

Composition 38 / A bad day   يــوم نـحـس .

*Write a composition describing one of your bad days.

I would like to write about a bad day. Yesterday was a bad day for me . Many things went wrong , thus causing me too much displeasure. First, I got up late and my father got angry because I would get late for school. Second , my car broke down , so I had to run to school . That was too hard for me. Third , at school I had an English test and I did not pass it , so the teacher got angry with me. Fourth , some students began to laugh at me because I failed the English test . That displeased me a lot. Finally , my football team lost a match , which saddened me a lot. It was really a bad day.

I suffered a lot yesterday , but I did not lose self- control. I felt that I was to blame for most of those bad things , so I promised to change my way of life. I experienced a bad day , but I learnt a useful lesson. It is not wrong to make a mistake , but it is wrong not to learn from that mistake.

* Key words :

get up يستيقظ / get angry يغضب / get late for يتأخر عنbreak
down تتعطل / broke down تعطلت   had to اضطررت
/ hard شاق – عسير / pass ينجح   fail يرسب في
/ laugh at (3) يسخر من   displease (4) يكدّر /
lost a match خسر مباراة
sad حزين - محزن / saddened أحزن / began بدؤوا cause
الغـم – الاستياء (1) displeasure /   يسبب
experience(2) يمر بـ - يلاقي
lose self-control يفقد السيطره الذاتيه mistake (5) خطأ – غلط

92

promised وعدت / learn يتعلم / learnt تعلم
a useful lesson درساً مفيداً

....

ملاحظة نطق: ١- د س بليجار / ٢- إكس بير يانص / ٣- لاف
٤- دس بليز / ٥- مس تيك

Composition 39 / Speed السرعة
* Write a composition about speed and what people
should do about it.

Nobody can deny that speed is dangerous. Speed is mad. Speed is to blame for the rising number of deaths and disabled people. We suffer a lot from road hogs because they cause horrible accidents. Road hogs not only kill innocent people, but also frighten children, thus making traffic too risky. Speed means death, thousands of people are killed in car accidents every year. We lose many innocent people due to car accidents.

Speed is dangerous, so we should fight it. Speed is a big problem, so we should do something to solve it. It is necessary to do something. It is mad to let road hogs kill innocent people. We should reduce speed. If we reduce speed, we will reduce accidents and losses. Less speed means safety. We should also follow the traffic rules if we want to fight speed. We must also improve our roads. We can build wide roads. Another thing, why not punish road hogs? If we do that, traffic will become safe.

In short, speed is wrong, and we can fight it. If we do something, we will see fewer accidents. If we drive safely, accidents will disappear. We want safety on our roads. We want accident-free roads. We should drive carefully to realize this noble goal.

* Key words :

speed السرعة / dangerous خطير / wrong خطأ   mad
جنون / suffer from يعاني من

93

road hogs مجانين السرعة
cause (1) / يسبب   horrible مخيف   / death
thousand (2) / ألف   lose (8) / نخسر   الموت – الوفاة
innocent (3) / برئ   due to (4) / بسبب   frighten (5) /
risky محفوفاً بالمخاطر / يرعب

improve نحسّن / is to blame for يكون مسؤولاً عن   rising number
العدد المتزايد (6)
reduce (7) / نقلل من   less speed / السرعة القليلة   mean تعني
safety السلامة / losses (9) خسائر   disappear
accident- free roads / طرق بلا حوادث   تختفي (10)
carefully بحذر / punish (12) نعاقب
to realize this noble goal (11) لكي نحقق هذا الهدف النبيل
.... ١- ملاحظة نطق :
كوز / ٢- ثاوزاند / ٣- إني سانت / ٤- ديو تو / ٥- فراي تن / ٦- راي زنق نم بار ٧- رد يوس / ٨- لـووز
/ ٩- لو سيـز / ١٠- دس أبيــر
١١- تو ريا لايـز ذس نوبل قوول/١٢- با نش

****

disabled people الناس المعاقين / fight نحارب / let نترك – ندع
solve نحل / follow نتبع / traffic rules (1) قوانين المرور   wide
roads طرق واسعة / fewer (2) أقل

* Fill in the spaces with suitable words :

1-   Speed is .... , so we should .... it .

2-   Speed means .... , so we should drive ....

3-   Speed is a big .... , so we should ….........… something to solve
     it.

4-   We suffer a lot from road …..........because they ....horrible
     accidents.

5-   Thousands of people are .... every year in car accidents.

6-   Road hogs kill .... people and frighten ....

94

7- Traffic has become too .... due to speed.

8- If we reduce speed , we will .... accidents and losses .

9- If we .... the traffic rules , we will see ....
accidents.

Composition 40 / Your school days
أيـــامـك الـــمـــدرســـية
× **Write a composition describing your school days .**

   My school days were terrible. I had a bad time at school , so I still have black memories of my early school days. My school days were bad in many ways. The school building was too old and the furniture so poor. The class-room was dirty all the time . The teachers were unkind because they hit the students , thus forcing many to drop out. We had to learn useless information ; some subjects were too difficult and the teachers could do nothing about them. The books were full of unnecessary information. We also had no sports facilities , so we did not play any games. The school canteen was the worst place on earth ; it scared me because it was full of flies and all sorts of rubbish.

   Nowadays I feel sorry about my school days because I was too helpless to do anything about them. I wish I had had   a good time at school . Today I feel happy because things have changed a lot for the better.

× **Key words :**

terrible مخيف – مقزز	/	black memory ذ كرى سوداء
memories ذكريات	/	building (1) المبنى
furniture (2) الأثاث	/	dirty (5) وسخ
class-room غرفة الصف	/	unkind قاسي – شديد
hit يضرب	/	force يجبر
drop out يتسرب	/	subjects (6) المواد difficult صعب
canteen المقصف	/	flies (4) ذباب
unnecessary information معلومات غير ضرورية		

scare يرعب / sports facilities (3) منشآت رياضية

feel sorry يشعر بالآسي / helpless عاجز / wish يتمنى

change for the better يتغير إلى الأفضل / all sorts of كل أنواع

....

ملاحـظة نطـق : ١- بيل دنق / ٢- فيرنتشَ / ٣- فاسيلي تيز / ٤- فلايز /

٥- ديـر تي / ٦- سـاب جكتس

* **language** لغـــة :

1- The furniture is too old ; we must change it.

* الأثاث قديم جداً . يجب أن نغيره .

* furniture ← هذه الكلمة مفردة مثل كلمة information

* This information is important . هذه المعلومات مهمة.

* This equipment costs a lot of money. هذه المعدات

تكلف الكثير من المال .

* The news has just reached me. لقد وصلني الخبر للتو .

2- Many students have dropped out of the school .

* كثير من الطلاب قد تسربوا من (تركوا) المدرسة.

3- I am **too helpless to** do anything.

* إني عاجز جداً لدرجة أنني لا أستطيع أن أفعل أي شئ .

He is **too fat to** run. إنه بدين جداً لدرجة أنه لا يستطيع أن يركض.

The question was **too difficult to** answer.

4- I wish I **went** to the party. يا ليتني أذهب إلى الحفلة .

I wish I **could buy** this car يا لتني أستطيع أن أشتري هذه السيارة

I wish I **had gone** to the party. يا ليتني ذهبت إلى الحفلة.

I wish I **had bought** that car. يا ليتني اشتريت تلك السيارة.

* **Fill in the spaces with suitable words :**

1- I have black .... of my early school days.

2- I .... a bad time at school .

3- My school days were terrible in many ....

4- The furniture was so ....and the building ....

5- The class-room was dirty ....

6- The teachers were .... to the students , which forced many students to ....

7- The school canteen .... me a lot because it was full of ....

Composition 41 / Introduce yourself قـدّم نفـسك

* **Write a composition introducing yourself to others.**

I want to tell you about myself. I have a positive character . I am a committed student with a high sense of responsibility , so I never do foolish things. I will finish my education soon. I am ambitious , so I am studying hard to get high marks . I am willing to join university to study information technology. I am good at English , Biology and Maths. In my free time , I go swimming and watch TV. I like travelling a lot ; I have travelled to many countries , so I know many languages. I like people who are friendly , helpful and open-minded. I am slim and fit because I take exercise regularly. I hate people who cheat and lie to others. I advocate freedom and peace because they lead to Man's prosperity. I respect people who fight for noble things. I respect people who fight vice and corruption.

I have a dream , so I am working hard to realize this dream. I do hope that I appeal to you.

* **Key words :**

positive (1) إيجابي / **character (2)** شخصية

committed ملتزم / / **fight** يحارب

a high sense of responsibility إحساس عال من المسؤولية

student (3) طالب / **education (4)** التعليم /

high marks درجات عالية / **willing** راغب

ambitious (5) طَموح / **join** يلتحق بـ

university الجامعة / travel يسافر travelling السفر
information technology تكنولوجيا المعلومات
language (6) لغة dream حلم / open- minded متفتح الذهن hate
يناصر advocate (7) يستهوي - يروق لـ appeal to / يكره
/ freedom الحرية lead to يؤدي إلى

Man's prosperity (8) رفاهية الإنسان / cheat (9) يغش lie to
السلام peace / يكذب على يناضل fight for
الرذيلة vice أشياء نبيلة noble things / من أجل
corruption (10) الفساد / dream حـلم

....

* ملاحظة نطـق: ١- بوزيتيق /٢- كاراك تا / ٣- ستيو دَنت / ٤- إديوكيشن / ٥- امبيشَس / ٦- لانق وج / ٧- ادڤوكيت / ٨- مانز بروس بيريتي / ٩- تشيت/ ١٠-كورا ابشن

* Language لغـة :

1- * I am committed to helping you. إني ملتزم بمساعدتك.
* We are committed to defending you. نحن ملتزمون
بالدفاع عنكم.

* I have a sense of responsibility . لدي إحساس بالمسؤولية.
* I am good at English. إني جيد في الإنجليزية .
* You always lie to me. أنت دائماً تكذب عليّ.
* Peace leads to prosperity. السلام يؤدي إلى الرفاهية.

2- * I like people who الذين are friendly.

98

* I hate people who smoke everywhere.

إني أكره الناس الذين يدخنون في كل مكان.

* I know the man who speaks English well .

إني أعرف الرجل الذي يتكلم الإنجليزية بشكل جيد.

ملاحظة :

who بمعنى (الذي – التي – الذين) تقوم مقام الاسم و يتبعها فعل .

Composition 42 / Applying for a job   Write a letter applying for a job .   أكتب رسالة طلب وظيفة

The Personnel Manager,   P.O .Box ......
Qatar Airways ,   Doha- Qatar.
P.O. Box .....
Doha - Qatar.   11th December 2003

Dear Sir ,

    I am writing to apply for the job of computer operator you advertised in *The Gulf Times* last Monday.

    I am a 30-year-old university graduate. I got my degree from Al- Salam University in 1995. I have a B.A. in computing .I have been working as a computer operator for 8 years. I have experience on IBM and Apple computers. I am getting a salary of Q.R. 5000 per month . I am hard-working and committed. I am good at dealing with all people. I speak Arabic and English well. I am interested in this job because I am looking for better working conditions.

    I look forward to hearing from you.

Yours faithfully,
Ali Nasser

* **Key words :**

طالب وظيفة applicant / طلب application / يتقدم لـ apply for

advertise يعلن عن   / advertisement (1) إعلان

degree درجة علمية   / graduate (2) خريج   experience (3) خبرة

/ work يعمل

salary راتب – معاش / get يحصل على / per month كل شهر

interested مهتم / look for يبحث عن

better working conditions (4) ظروف عمل أفضل

 look forward to يتطلع إلى

....

ملاحظة نطق: ١- أدڤيـر تايزمنت / ٢ قراج يو وت / ٣- إكس بيريانس

٤- ويـركـنـق كـون ديـشنز

* Language لغـة :

1- I have been working *for* 8 years .

   He has been playing *for* hours .

* إني أعمل منذ ٨ سنوات .

* إنه يلعب منذ ساعات .

for ——← بعدها تأتي طول المدة التي قضاها الشخص وهو يؤدي عملاً ما

ويجب أن يكون الفعل في الشكل الرابع مسبوقاً بــــ ↓

(have been أو has been)

2- I look forward to hearing from you. يتطلع إلى

   ↓

* يأتي بعدها فعل شكل رابع بمثابة اسم .

3- I am good at   dealing with people .

   ↓

* يأتي بعدها فعل شكل رابع بمثابة اسم لأنها حرف جر.

* Fill in the spaces with suitable words :

1- I want to .... this job because I want   a

    .... salary.

2- He is .... in this job because the .... is high.

3- I am a university ....; I got my .... from Qatar

    University in 1990.

4- I .... doing this job .... 5 years.

100

5- She has been .... the dishes for half an hour.

6- They have been .... for a long time.

7- She is good .... cooking and painting.

8- I look forward to .... you at the City Centre.

9- I am looking for better working ....

10- We need to employ نوظف three people for this job.

    I think that we should .... the job in a

    newspaper.

Composition 43 / A good day .

* **Write a composition describing a good day .**

    I would like to write about a good day. Yesterday was the best day

of my life. I had many pleasant things that day. First , a friend called to

tell me that I passed my final exams with high marks. That news pleased

me   a lot because I could join university to study journalism .

Second , my father promised to buy me a new car , thus realizing a long-

waited dream . Third , my brother offered to take me to London with

him . That was really great news because I would have a chance to develop

my English . Fourth , my football team beat Al-Hilal football team 3: 0 ,

thus winning the Gulf football cup . Finally , my sister

gave birth to a boy . That was the best news because my sister had

five daughters!

I thanked Allah for those pleasant things , which gave me a sense

of confidence . Good news refreshes and encourages me a lot.

* **Key words :**

pleasant (1) سار - مفرح	/	the best day أفضل يوم
called اتصل	/	passed نجح في
high marks درجات عالية	/	join يلتحق بـ
final exams الامتحانات النهائي	/	pleased أسعد
university الجامعة	/	journalism (2) صحافة
promised وعد	/	buy (3) يشتري
offered عرض	/	great news خبر رائع
team فريق	/	beat يهزم - هزم
win يفوز بـ	/	won فاز بـ
cup كأس	/	gave birth to أنجبت
daughter (4) ابنة	/	realize يحقق
a sense of confidence إحسا س بالثقة		
a long- waited dream حلم طال انتظاره		
refresh تنعش	/	encourage (5) تشجع

....

* ملاحظة نطق : 1- بليزَنت / 2- جيرنالزم / 3- باي /

4- دوتار/ 5- إنـكا رج

(a) وصـف مـنظـر / A view / Composition 44
* Write a composition describing a view.

I want to describe a view yesterday . Yesterday morning   I was walking along the Doha Corniche. It was 5 o'clock in the early morning. The weather was fantastic; visibility was excellent and there was a fresh breeze of air. I saw a nice view . I saw children running everywhere. They were having a good time. I saw a father playing football with his three kids. I saw   a group of people sailing in a boat. They were singing and dancing. I saw men and women walking and jogging . They wanted to lose **weight** . They wanted **to get fit** . I saw hundreds of birds flying everywhere . I saw a green area with a variety of colourful flowers and palm-trees.

There were tens of palm-trees that made the view was impressive. The Corniche is a good **area for picnicking** . I can say that this area has made walking **a great pleasure** . I advise people to come to this place. They will enjoy it. I hope that people will benefit from this wonderful area.

* **Key words :**

describe a view (1) يصف منظراً   / visibility (2) الرؤية

a fresh breeze نسيم عليل   / jog يـهـرول

lose weight (3) يخسـس الوزن   / get fit يكتسب لياقة

103

area (4)	منطقة	/ variety (5) تشكيلة
palm- trees (6)	أشجار النخيل	/ impressive رائع – مؤثر
picnic (7)	نزهة – يتنزه	/ picnicking التنزه
a great pleasure (8)	متعة كبيرة	/ advise ينصح
palm-trees (9)	أشجار النخيل	

....

٥- قارايا ملاحظة نطق : ١- ڤيو / ٢- ڤيزي بيليتي / ٣- لووز ويت / ٤- إيريا /
تي / ٦- بام تـريز / ٧- بيك نك / ٨- بليجا (ر) /
٩- بـام تـريـز

Composition 45 / A view (b)
* Write a composition describing a view :

The weather was excellent last Friday when I was climbing the highest mountain in the world. When I reached the top , I was extremely excited. What impressed me was the beautiful view I saw. It was the most beautiful view I had ever seen . The top of Everest was covered with white snow. Snow was everywhere. When I looked below , I saw a breath-taking valley ; it was too deep and water was running through . I looked left to find slopes covered with tall , green trees. I looked right to see a round lake at the top of another mountain range with thousands of lovely, colourful birds that I had never seen before. When I looked behind me , I saw a bees' hive where bees are working together for the good of their hive meaning to send a message to people whose hostilities have ruined the beauty of nature.
I enjoyed the view a lot , so I will never forget it.

* Key words :

....

view (1) منظر	/ excellent (2) ممتاز	/ climb يتسلق

104

reach (3) يصل إلى / top قمة / mountain (4) جبل
excited سررت / impressed أسرني / snow ثلج
covered with مغطى بـ / breath-taking أخاذ / valley وادي
slopes سفوح / lake بحيرة / bees النحل
hostility (5) عداوة / hive خلية / message رسالة
for the good of لخير – لمصلحة / peacefully بشكل سلمي
mean يقصدون بذلك / ruin (6) يدمر
beauty (7) جمال / nature (8) الطبيعة

....

ملاحظة تطق : ١- قيو / ٢- اكسي لنت / ٣- ريتش / ٤- ماونتن /
٥ - هوس تيليتي / ٦- ري ون / ٧- بيوتي / ٨- ني تشار /

Composition 46 / Studying abroad الدراسة بالخارج
* **Write a composition about this topic :**
    " **Studying abroad - advantages and disadvantages.** "

    I want to tell you about studying abroad. Some people are for it. Others are against it. It is useful to know the different opinions. Some people are for studying abroad because they think that people benefit a lot from that. The advantages are certain . First , if you study abroad , you will learn many good things . You will learn how to rely on yourself . You will also get first-hand information about other countries. Second , if you study abroad , you will get real education. The education system is totally different from ours. The education system abroad is not based on memorization . It is based on analysis. Third , the fans say that studying abroad can improve your way of thinking because you can freely exchange ideas with others.

    But other people are against studying abroad. Nobody can deny the disadvantages. If you study abroad, you will lose a lot. First, if you study abroad , you may learn strange ideas . These ideas may spoil your way of thinking, making you hostile to your people's way of life. Second , if you study abroad , you will miss your family. Many students suffer from a sense of alienation . The parents worry a lot about their children. Another thing, Some students cannot adapt to the new way of life , so they have to return home . Studying abroad is also too expensive ; it costs too much money. Only rich people can afford it!

We can say that studying abroad has advantages and disadvantages. It is good to study abroad , but you have to take care lest you should get into trouble. If you follow this advice , studying abroad becomes a pleasure. If you ignore this advice , studying abroad becomes a disaster.

* Key words :

abroad بالخارج / advantages (1) مزايا / disadvantages مساوئ
for مؤيد / against ضد / real education تعليم حقيقي
totally كلياً / system نظام / based on قائم على memorization
الحفظ غيباً (2) / analysis (3) التحليل fans مؤيدون /
way of thinking طريقة التفكير
miss يحن إلى / a sense of alienation الشعور بالوحشة
worry يقلق / parents الوالدان
expensive (4) غال / cost يكلف
take care يأخذ الحيطة / ignore يتجاهل
follow this advice يتبع هذه النصيحة / pleasure (5) متعة disaster (6) كارثة
/ adapt to(7) يتكيف مع hostile (8)
معادي

* Fill in the spaces with suitable words :

1- Studying abroad has advantages and ....

2- Some people are .... studying abroad. They say that we benefit a lot from it.

3- The advantages are .... If you study abroad , you will get real ....

4- Our education system is based on ....

5- The education system abroad is based on ....

6-   Some companies prefer to give jobs to people with degrees from
     ....

7-   Some people are .... studying abroad. If you study abroad , you
     will lose a lot.

8-   If you study abroad , you will .... your family.

9-   The parents will .... about their children who study abroad.

10-Studying abroad is too ....; only rich people
     can afford it.

....

مـلاحـظـة نـطـق : 1- أد قـان تـجـز / 2- ميمـو رايـزيـشن
3- أنا ليـسـس / 4- إكس بنسـق / 5- بليجـا ر / 6- دي زاس تار
7- أد ا بـت / 8- هـوس تـا يـال .

Composition 47 /   Staying with an English family.

● **Write a composition about this topic :**

   " **Staying with an English family.**"   الإقامـة
            مـع عـائـلة إنجلـيـزيـة

   I want to tell you about students staying with an English family. Some
people are for it. Others are against it.

   Some students prefer to stay with an English family while studying in
England. They say that they benefit a lot from it. First , you can improve your
English because you mix with native speakers most of the time. Second , you
will learn more about the English way of life , so you will enrich your
experience. Third , the English family will help you solve many problems . The
family environment will make you feel at home .

   But other people are against staying with an English family. They say
that it is dangerous to live with an English family. If you do that , you will face
many problems. First , you may learn strange things which endanger your
culture. Second , the English family may affect you badly ; they may teach you
things that are not accepted in your country.

   In short , it is not bad to stay with an English family , but you should
take care . I hope that you will follow this advice. If you follow this advice
, staying with an English

family becomes a pleasure . If you ignore it , you will bring yourself a disaster.

* Key words :

prefer   يفضّل   /   improve   تحسّن   /   mix with   تختلط مع

native speakers   الناطقين الأصليين   /   way of life   طريقة الحياة

family environment(1) البيئة العائلية / experience (2) خبرة – تجربة

solve   يحل   /   feel at home   يشعر بالألفة

endanger   يعرّض للخطر   /   strangeالثقافة culture (3) غريبة

/ accepted   مقبولة   /   affect   يؤثر في   take care يأخذ الحيطة

/ follow this advice   تتبع هذه النصيحة

bring yourself   تجلب لنفسك   /   disaster (4) كارثة

* مــلاحـظـة ....

نـطـق : 1- إن ڤـايرو منـت / 2- اكـس بـير يـانس / 3-كـال تـشار/ 4- دي زاس تـار

* Fill in the spaces with suitable words :

1-   Some students .... to stay with an English family.

2-   Other students are .... staying with an English family.

3-   If you stay with an English family , you will .... your
      English.

4-   You mix with .... speakers of English , so you can improve your
      English.

5-   If you stay with an English family , you will feel ....

6-   The English family will help you .... many problems.

7-   It is wrong to .... with an English family while studying in
      England.

8-   If you stay with an English family , you will .... a lot .The
      English family may .... you badly. They may
      .... you strange things.

9-   If you stay with an English family , you will ....
      your culture.

10-   If you want to stay with an English family , you should

take …….............. . If you .... this advice ,
you will .... yourself many problems.

● **Re-order these words to make sentences :**

1- family / staying / am / English / an / with / against / I
………………...……………………............……………..................

2- not / is / to stay / wrong / It / an English family / with / ,
but / is / wrong / it / to do that / your culture / at the
expense of على حساب
………............………………………………………………………..

3- new / get / an English family / experience / stay / you / you /
with / When / stay / a /
……………………………………………………………………..

Composition 48 / Journalism الـصـحـافـة
* **Write a composition about journalism .**

I want to tell you about the importance of journalism. Nobody can
deny that journalism plays a key role in everyday life. We need free journalism
a lot because we benefit a lot from it. The advantages of free journalism are
great. First , free newspapers affect people a lot in the sense that they can shape
public opinion. They provide people with information . Second , free newspapers
encourage freedom of expression ; people have a chance to express their ideas
freely . Third , free journalism means that we have real democracy . It is useful
to have both democracy and free journalism . If we have democracy and free
journalism , we can develop our country. Thanks to democracy , free journalism
can flourish a lot. Fourth , thanks to free journalism , we can discuss
and criticize everything freely.

In short , free journalism is useful , so we should fight for it. Free journalism is a noble goal worth fighting for. Once we realize this goal , we should use free journalism well. Journalists should realize the fact that they have limits that they should not exceed. I am for free journalism , but I am against any misuse of free journalism.

* Key words :

play a key role in يلعب دوراً رئيسياً / importance أهمية / journalism (1) الصحافة / advantages مزايا

freedom / encourage (2) يشجع provide يزود public opinion الرأي العام / يؤثر في affect

realize يحقق - يدرك / حدود limits / يستحق worth حرية التعبير of expression (3)

freely بحرية / بشكل ideas أفكار يعبر عن express / فرصة chance / إساءة استخدام misuse

real democracy (4) ديمقراطية develop ينمي -يطور / حر

discuss (6) بفضل thanks to flourish (5) يزدهر / حقيقية

يتجاوز exceed (8) / ينتقد criticize (7) يناقش

against ضد / مؤيد for / يناضل من أجل for fight

ملاحظة نطق: ١- جيرنالزم / ٢- انكا رج / ٣- فريدم أ ڤ اكسبريشن /

٤- ريال ديموك راسي/٥- فلا رش / ٦- دس كاس / ٧- كريتي سايز /

٨ - إكسيد

Composition 49 / The environment البيئة .

*Write a composition about this topic :
" Man and Nature (the environment) ."

Nobody can deny that nature is useful . Nature provides Man with all the necessary things that he needs to live . First, people get light and heat from the Sun. The ozone layer protects people from the Sun's harmful rays. Second , people get food and drugs from trees and plants. Trees make oxygen for people. Third , we get fresh water from rivers and lakes. Nature is useful , so we should protect it. If we protect it , we protect life. Nobody can ignore this fact.

But Man is destroying the environment. First , Man is burning big amounts of coal, oil and gas , thus increasing the amount of CO_2 in the atmosphere. The CO_2 layer traps the Sun's heat , thus increasing the earth's temperature . Second , Man is making some harmful chemicals that damage the ozone layer. Third , Man is cutting trees . Man is destroying nature , thus causing too much pollution.

Pollution is a big problem ; we should do something to solve it. We should save energy ; less energy means less pollution. If we reduce energy , we reduce pollution. Besides , we can re-use cans, bottles and paper to save energy. We can use small cars. We can use unleaded petrol in our cars. We can replace plastic bags with paper ones. If we do that, we will reduce pollution.

In short, Man is destroying nature. It is wrong to destroy nature. If you destroy nature, you destroy life. Man is causing pollution, but he can solve this problem. We should fight pollution. We do not need pollution. We need a clean environment, so we should fight for it.

*Key words :

nature (1) الطبيعة / environment (2) البيئة /
provide توفر- تزود / reduce يقلل من /
all the necessary things جميع الأشياء الضرورية / light
الضوء / heat الحرارة coal الفحم
the ozone layer طبقة الأوزون / trap يحبس / protect تحمي harmful
rays الأشعة الضارة / plants النباتات / drugs (3) عقاقير destroy يدمر
/ burn (4) يحرق /
amount (5) كمية / increase يرفع من -يزيد
atmosphere (6) الغلاف الجوي / cause (7) يسبب temperatue (8)
درجة الحرارة / pollute يلوث
pollution (9) التلوث / chemicals (10) مواد كيماوية
damage يتلف- يخرب / save يوفر -يقتصد في

-
* ملاحظة نطق : ١- نيتشا(ر) / ٢- إن ڤايرومنت / ٣- دراقز / ٤- بيرن /٥- أما
ونت / ٦- أتـموس فيـر / ٧- كـوو ز /٨- تيـم بـريتـشا ر
٩ - بـل يـو شـن / ١٠- كـيـمي كـا لـز

****

* Fill in the spaces with suitable words:
1- Man is getting from nature all the ....things to his life on the earth.

112

2- The Sun provides people with .... and ....

3- The .... protects people from the Sun's .... rays.

4- People get .... and .... from trees and plants.

5- Trees do a very important job ; they .... CO_2 into oxygen.

6- It is wrong to .... nature. If we .... it , we destroy life.

7- Man is .... the environment ; he is burning big .... of coal , oil and gas.

8- The amount of CO is .... ; this is bad . The CO_2

Composition 50 / Finding new energy sources .

إيجاد مصادر جديدة للطاقة

Write a composition about this topic :

" Why we need to find other energy sources."

    I want to tell you about the need to find new energy sources. Energy is necessary to Man. We are getting energy from coal , oil and gas , but these energy sources are non- renewable and pollute the environment. These sources will run out one day , so it is important to find other sources.

    People are trying to get energy from the Sun. Solar energy is renewable , cheap and safe . But the Sun cannot provide people with energy all the time. People are building windmills to generate electricity , but the wind power is not available all the time . People are trying to use water to generate electricity . All these alternatives cannot provide people with all the energy they need , so it becomes necessary to use the nuclear power. We can generate big amounts of electricity by using the nuclear energy , but nuclear energy has a big disadvantage : it gives off harmful radiations.

    In short , we need new energy sources because the present ones are either bad for the environment or they are non-renewable . We should work hard to find a safe energy source.

   * Key words :

energy source (1) / مصدر للطاقة / coal الفحم
non- renewable غير متجددة / pollute تلوث
the environment البيئة / run out تنضب
solar energy الطاقة الشمسية / windmill طاحونة هوائية
generate يولد / amount كمية
electricity (2) الكهرباء / alternatives (3) البدائل
nuclear power الطاقة النووية / disadvantage (4) عيب
give off تصدر / radiations إشعاعات
present الحالية / either ..... or إما أن ...... أو

....

ملاحظة نطـق : ١- إنر جي سورس / ٢- إليك تري سيتي / ٣-
أول تيـر ناتـفز / ٤- دس أد قـا ن تيـج /

● **Fill in the spaces with suitable words :**

1- We .... energy a lot.   2- We get
.... from oil , gas and ....

3- Oil and gas are energy .... , but they are non-
.... They will ....one day.

4 - Oil , gas and coal are bad for the ....

5- Oil ,gas and coal .... the environment.

6- We need to find new .... sources.

7- We can get .... from the Sun.

8- Solar energy is .... , safe and ....

9- We cannot get solar ....all the time.   10- We can get
energy .... the wind.

11- We can use windmills to .... electricity.

12- Both the sun and wind cannot ....people with all
   the energy they need all the time.

● **Re-order these words to make sentences:**

1- can / power / electricity / to / the / use / **We** / nuclear /
   generate / of / amounts / huge /
   ....

2- power / cause / stations /others / pollution / than / **Nuclear** / less /

....

3- one / power / big / got / **Nuclear** / disadvantage / has /

....

4- find / that / for / should / the / energy sources / new / **We** / are / environment / less harmful /

....

Composition 51 / Oil الـــنــفــط
* **Write a composition about oil.**

Nobody can deny that the discovery of oil has changed our life a lot. The advantages of oil are great. First , some countries produce oil and sell it to others , thus earning a lot of money. Oil has become the main source of income in many countries. Thanks to oil , the standard of living has improved a lot in the oil-producing countries. Second , oil is an important energy source . We use petrol to drive cars , planes and trains. We use oil to drive machinery in factories. We use oil to generate electricity. Third , oil is the backbone of modern industry. Oil is a raw material on which many industries depend. Oil is used for making things like perfumes , ink , clothes , paints and tyres . Fourth , many products are derived from crude oil . We get petrol , grease ,gasoline , kerosene and many other things .

We can say that oil has changed our life for the better ; it has made our life easy and comfortable. Oil is so valuable that we should stop using it as a source of energy. Oil is most essential to many industries that make our life easy. Oil is playing a very important role in our life , so we should use it well. The world's strong economies depend closely on oil , so the Super Powers are struggling to dominate the oil-rich countries by all means.

*Key words :

يكسب earn / غيّر changed / اكتشاف discovery

رئيسي main / تنتج produce (1) /

يحرّك drive /

تحسّن improved / مصدر للدخل source of income (2)

آلات machinery (3) / مستوى المعيشة standard of living

نولد generate / مصانع factories / مصنع factory

دهانات paints / العمود الفقري backbone الكهرباء electricity /

العطر perfume / الصناعات industries الصناعة industry (4) /

الحبر ink / العطر perfume / يعتمد على depend on /

قيّم –ثمين valuable (5) / اطارات tyres /

products (7) مهما كلف الأمر by all means / دور role / ضروري essential (6)

يتم are derived (8) / الزيت الخام crude oil منتجات – مشتقات

/ اشتقاقها / اقتصاد economy (9) economies اقتصاديات

closely بصورة وثيقة / The Super Powers (10) القوى العظمى

struggle (11) تتصارع / to dominate (12) لكي تهيمن على

....

ملاحظة نطق: ١- برود يوس / ٢- سورس أق انكام / ٣- ماشينا ري /
٤- انداست ري / ٥- ڤاليوا بول / ٦- إيسن شال / ٧- برو دكتس/ ٦- إيسن شال
/ ٧- برو دكتس / ٨- دي ـرايڤد / ٩- إكونو مي/
١٠ -سوبر باورز / ١١- ستـراقل / ١٢ – دو مينيت

116

Composition 52 / The seatbelt حـزام الأمـان

*Write a composition about the importance of the seat-belt.

I want to shed light on the importance of the seat -belt. The seat-belt is useful , so we should use it . If we use it , we will benefit a lot. Nobody can deny the advantages. First , we need the seat-belt to protect lives. The seat- belt means safety. Second , we use the seat-belt to save lives. If you have an accident , the seat-belt can save your life. Third , the seat-belt can reduce losses. The seat-belt does not cost a lot , but it means a lot. If you do not use it , you may pay a high price for that . You may lose your life for not using the seat-belt.

The seat-belt is useful , so I advise everybody to use it. Everybody has to make sure that they have a seat-belt in their cars . Your life is dear , so why not protect it ? I think that the police should punish people who refuse to use the seat-belt . Let's use the seat- belt. We may save a life !

In short , we want to save lives . We should use the seat-belt to realize this noble goal . We want safety. The seat-belt is not an end in itself , but it is a means. The seat -belt is a means of realizing a noble goal , safety.

* **Key words :**

shed light on يسلط الضوء على / deny ينكر   advantages المزايا

protect يحمي   /   a life روح- حياة شخص

lives (1) أرواح   /   save ينقذ / mean يعني

safety السلامة   / reduce (2) يقلل من / loss خسارة   losses الخسائر

/ dear عزيزة   / cost يكلف   punish(3)

يعاقب   /   refuse يرفض /   means وسيلة   realize (4)

يحقق   / an end غاية / make sure يتأكد pay a high price يدفع

ثمناً غالياً

....

* ملاحظــة نـطــق : ١- لايـڤز / ٢- رديوس / ٣- بـا نيـش / ٤- ريا لايز

* **Language   لـغـة** :

1 **Using** the seat- belt does not cost a lot.

↓ بمعنى استخدام –اسم

×

2- We should punish **people** . **People** refuse to use the seat - belt.

We should punish people who الذين refuse to use the seat- belt.

3- The seat- belt is **the means of realizing** this noble goal.

إن حزام الأمان هو وسيلة لتحقيق هذا الهدف النبيل .

* **the means of**   (وسيلة لـ)- يتبعها فعل شكل رابع بمثابة اسم

* **Fill in the spaces with suitable words :**

1- I like people who ....

2- I hate people who ....

3- This is my means of .... my goals.

4- I am for .... the seatbelt.

5- .... the seatbelt can save your life.

6- I ....people to use the seatbelt while driving.

118

7- If we use the seatbelt , we will .... losses.

8- If you don't use the seatbelt , the police will .... you.

9-If you do not use the seatbelt , you will endanger تعرّض للخطر

your ....

10- .... a life is a noble goal..

Composition 53 / An opening speech   خطاب افتتاح

مشروع ما

* Write a composition about this topic :

"A new town has been built somewhere in your country .
The Minister of Housing opened it and made a speech at the opening
ceremony." Write the Minister's speech.

Ladies and gentlemen ,

I am happy to speak to you . I am proud to open this modern
town . This project is a great achievement. You will benefit a lot from it , so you
should take care of it. This project provides houses and facilities for you , so it
will solve the housing problem. We have modern shopping centres , where you
can do your shopping easily. We have traffic- free areas , where you can walk
safely. We have many green areas , where you can relax. We have wide roads ,
so we do not have traffic jams. We have health and education facilities
everywhere. The town is well –designed so that people can have easy access to
the facilities.

I assure you that this project will change your life for the
better . It will give our country a world lead in the field of
architecture. Thanks to this project , our country will flourish

119

a lot , so we should take care of it. I hope that you will have   a sense of
responsibility for this important project . If you take care of it . it will relieve you
a lot.

* Key words :

Minister of Housing وزير الإسكان /made a speech (1) ألقى خطاباً
opening ceremony (2) حفل إفتتاح /   proud (3)   فخور
achievement (4)   إنجاز   /   take care of   يهتم بـ
provide   يوفر   / facility منشأة / facilities منشأت
traffic-free خالٍ من المرور / areas مناطق / project المشروع
relax   يستجم -يستريح   / wide واسع / assure (5) يؤكد لـ
traffic jams   اختناقات مرورية   / field (6)   مجال
health facilities   منشأت صحية   /

education facilities منشأت تعليمية /
well- designed   مصممة تصميماً جيداً
a world lead   مكانة الصدارة في العالم / easy access سهولة الوصول
architecture (7)   فن العمارة   / flourish (8)   يزدهر

....
ملاحظة نطــق: ١- سبيـتش   ٢- سيروموني / ٣- براود / ٤- أتشيق منت /   ٥- أشور/ ٦-
فيلـد / ٧- أركي تكتـشار / ٨- فلارش

* Fill in the spaces with suitable words :

1- The .... of Housing opened a modern town and made a
   speech at the opening ....

2- This project is a great ....

3- Nobody can .... that you will benefit a lot from it.

4- I advise you to .... this project.

5- This town will .... your housing problems.

6- This town has .... like schools , hospitals and parks.

7- We have green .... , where we can relax .

8- We have .... areas , where we can walk safely.

9- We do not have traffic .... because we have wide roads.

10- We have health and education .... everywhere.

* Re-order these words to make sentences :

1- for / will / project / life /change / better / the /**This** / your

....

2- our / will / **This** / a world lead / country / project /
give /

....

3- our /a lot / flourish /this /**Thanks to**/ will / country / project /

....

Composition 54 / A new shopping centre   مـركـز
                        تـسـوق جـديـد

● **Write a composition about a new shopping centre that has opened in your area.**

        I want to tell you my opinion of the new shopping centre in my area. It is a great achievement . Nobody can deny the advantages. First , the centre is not crowded , so you can do your shopping easily. Second , everything is cheap . If you do your shopping here , you will save a lot of money. Third , the centre is close to houses , so people can reach it easily. Fourth , the salesmen are friendly and helpful , so people can get things easily. Fifth , the centre is open around the clock , which means that people can do shopping at any time. Sixth, The centre provides a home- delivery service which relieves the handicapped a lot. Finally , thanks to the big number of the car-parks , customers do not have parking problems .

        In short , this centre is wonderful. Thanks to it , people do not have any shopping problem.. In fact , it has made shopping a great pleasure.

If you come to this centre , you will enjoy shopping here.

* Key words :

opinion رأي / achievement إنجاز / advantages مزايا
crowded مزدحم / shopping التسوق / cheap (1) رخيص
save توفر / close to قريب من / reach (2) يصل إلى
easily (3) بسهولة / salesmen الباعة / number (4) العدد
has made لقد جعل / pleasure (5) متعة / customers (6) زبائن
around the clock على مدار الساعة / provide يوفر
a home – delivery service (7) خدمة التوصيل للبيوت
relieve تريح / تخفف من عناء the
handicapped (8) المعاقين

....

* ملاحظة نطق : ١- تشيب /٢- ريتش / ٣- إيزيلي / ٤- نمبار / ٥- بليجار /٦-
كاستومارز / ٧- دي ليڤا ري / ٨- هاندي كا بد .

*Fill in the spaces with suitable words :

1-   I want to tell you my ....of this centre.

2-   It is a .... achievement .

3-   Nobody can deny the ....

4-   I advise you to ....your shopping here. If you do that , you will
       benefit a lot. You will .... a lot of money.

5-   The centre is not .... , so you can do your shopping easily.

6-   The centre is .... houses . You can .... it easily.

7-   The salesmen are .... and ....

8-   There is a big .... of car-parks , so we do not have any parking
       ....

9-   Thanks to this centre , we do not have any .... problem.

10-   This centre has .... shopping a great ....

* Re-order these words to make sentences :

1- advise / to / you / shopping / do / your / here / I /

122

....

2- that / will / hope / this advice / I / you / follow /

....

3- get /things / will /prices أسعار / at / good / cheap / **You**

....

4- have / customers / because / many / **We**/ so / we / a lot / sell

....

5 madc / a / pleasure / have / **We** / shopping / great

....

Composition 55 / A new ring – road

طـــريـــق دائـــري جــديــد

* Write a composition about the new ring-road that has just opened in your town.

    I want to tell you my opinion of the new ring-road . It is a great achievement . Nobody can deny the advantages. First , it has solved many traffic problems . Thanks to the new ring-road , we no longer have any traffic jams. Traffic has become easy and safe. Second , the new ring-road has reduced the number of car accidents. The drop in accidents means a drop in losses. This gives people a sense of safety. Third , thanks to the zebra- crossings , children and old people can cross the road safely. Fourth , the road has enough traffic signs that guide road users , which enables them to reach their destinations easily.

    I think that this ring-road has improved the traffic situation in our town a lot , so we should use it well . I am sure that this ring- road will make driving a great pleasure. We need easy, safe traffic , so we should use this ring-road well to realize this goal.

* Key words :

ring- road / طريق دائري / achievement / إنجاز / deny / ينكر
advantages / مزايا / solved / حل / made / جعل
no longer / لم نعد / traffic jams / اختناقات مرورية
traffic / حركة المرور / become / أصبحت / drop / ينخفض –هبوط
reduced / قلل من / means / يعني / improve / يحسّن
يمكّن / enable / losses / الخسائر / traffic signs (1) / إشارات مرورية
will make / سيجعل / a sense of safety / إحساس بالأمان / zebra- crossings
يمكّن / enable / مناطق عبور المشاة
the traffic situation (2) / الوضع المروري / sure (3) / متأكد
pleasure (4) / متعة / guide (5) / يرشد
road users / مستخدموا الطريق / destination (6) / الجهة المقصودة

....

* ملاحظة نطق : ١- ترافك سا ينز / ٢- ذا ترافك سيتيو ويشن / ٣- شور /
٤- بليجار / ٥- قا يد / ٦- ديٍـستي نيـشن

* Fill in the spaces with suitable words :

1- A new .... has just opened in our town.

2- I think that it is a great ....

3- Nobody can deny the ....

4- You will .... a lot from this ring-road , so you should use it well.

5- Thanks to this ring-road , the traffic situation has .... a lot.

6- Traffic has .... easy and safe.

7- This ring-road has .... the number of accidents.

8- Thanks to this ring-road , the number of .... has dropped
sharply انخفض بشكل حاد .

9- The road has enough road signs which .... road users to reach
their .... easily.

10- The drop in accidents gives people a .... of safety.

* Re-order these words to make sentences :

1- will / ring-road/ your / change /This /the /for / better / life/

....

124

2- you / make / to / road /of/ advise / this / the most / **I**

....

3- make / a / driving / great / road /pleasure / will / **This**

....

4- solve / ring-road / traffic / will / **This** / problems / many

....

5- become / **Thanks to** / traffic / ring-road / has / easy / this /

.... 6- a sense

of safety / **People** / because / has / traffic signs / the

road / many / road / the / have /

....

Composition 56 / The new airport المطار الجديد

● **Write a composition about the new airport that has just opened in your country.**

I want to tell you about the new airport that has just opened in my country. It is a great achievement. Nobody can deny that it has many advantages. First , it will solve many transport problems. Thanks to this airport , people can travel easily everywhere . As a result , air transport will flourish a lot , thus improving the economy of the country. Second , this airport will encourage businessmen to travel a lot . This will give a boost to trade . Third , more tourists will come to our country. This will make **Qatar** a tourist country. Fourth , the new airport can receive giant planes . This will increase the number of flights. Finally , this airport is located outside the town . This means that people will not suffer from noise.

I am confident that this airport will give our country a world lead in the field of air transport. Besides , it will change our life for the better because it will make travelling a great pleasure. People need easy , comfortable travelling , so we should use this airport to realize this goal.

airport / مطار / achievement (1) انجاز / deny ينكر
advantages / مزايا / air transport النقل الجوي travel يسافر / as a
result (2) ونتيجة لذلك / improve يحسّن / flourish (3) يزدهر / economy (4) اقتصاد / make يجعل /
encourage (5) يشجع
businessmen (6) رجال الأعمال / give a boost to (7) لـ يعطي دفعة
trade (8) التجارة / tourists (9) سياح confident واثق / a tourist
country بلد سياحي / receive (10) يستقبل / field مجال /
travelling السفر travelling السفر / giant planes (11) طائرات عملاقة

increase (12) يرفع –يزيد من / flight (13) رحلة جوية /
a world lead مكانة الصدارة في العالم / pleasure (14) متعة
located يقع / suffer from يعاني من / noise ضوضاء

....

ملاحظة نطق : ١- أتـشيـﭫ منـت / ٢- آز أري زالـت / ٣- فلا رش / ٤-
إكونومي/ ٥- إنكا رج / ٦- بزنس من / ٧- أبوست / ٨- تريد / ٩- تورستس ١٠-
ريسيﭫ/ ١١- جا يا نـت / ١٢ - إنك ريس / ١٣ – فلاي تـس / ١٤- بليجار
/

* Fill in the spaces with suitable words :

1- The new airport is a great ....

2- This airport has many .... It has ....

many transport problems.

3- Thanks to this airport , air transport has ....

a lot.

4- Thanks to this airport, the ....of flights

has increased a lot.

5- The new airport will .... businessmen to travel

126

a lot.

6- Thanks to this airport , trade will ....a lot.

7-Thanks to this airport , the number of .... will

increase . This will give a .... to tourism. 8- Thanks to this

airport , people can .... easily

everywhere.

9- This airport will give a boost to the .... of the

country.

10-This airport will make traveling a great ....

Composition 57 / The reporter المراسـل الصحفي.

● **Write a composition about the reporter.**

I want to tell you about the reporter. Nobody can deny that the reporter is doing an important job. He provides people with information about events that take place here and there. He also gives people an analysis of some important events , thus affecting their reactions .

The reporter's job is risky because he may have to travel to a war area , where he may lose his life. In some cases , the reporter's views do not appeal to the authority , so the authority may imprison him. Some countries do not allow reporters to tell the truth . Honest reporters have problems with the authority because they express ideas that displease the authority . In many cases , anti- authority reporters are detained and tortured.

We need honest reporters . We expect reporters to tell the truth. We want reporters to report events frankly . We respect reporters who give people facts. We hate reporters who hide facts from people and who tell lies to please the authority.

In short , people need facts , not lies . Reporters should be aware of this fact. Reporters should realize this fact. If they do that , they will maintain freedom of expression. Reporters should realize that they have limits they should not exceed. They should do their job without libelling others.

● **Key words :**

reporter مراسل صحفي / provide يزود / events (1) أحداث take place

ردة reaction (3) يؤثر في affect / analysis (2) تحليل / تحدث

قد may have to يدرك realize / محفوف بالمخاطر risky (4) / فعل

يطعن - (5) libel / a war area منطقة حروب / يضطر إلى أن

يـشّـهـر بـ / in some cases في بعض الحالات / views (6) أراء /

appeal to تروق لـ / authority (7) السلطة imprison (8)

أن ينقل report / / نتوقع من expect / تسجن

يقول الصدق (10) tell the truth / أمين- شريـف honest (9)

frankly بصراحة / respect (11) نحترم / report أن ينقل

hide يُخفي / to please لكي يرضي / facts الحقائق /

يـصون- maintain / على علمٍ بـ - على وعى بـ aware of

يساعد على استمرار / / tell lies (12) يحكي أكاذيب -يقول الكذب

128

freedom of expression (13) حدود limits / حرية التعبير

exceed (14) يتجاوز / anti- authority معادون للسلطة

are tortured (15) يتم تعذيبهم / are detained يتم اعتقالهم

ملاحظة نطق : ١- إقـنـتـس / ٢- أنا ليـسـس / ٣- ري أكشن / ٤- رسكي /

٥- لاي بل /٦- فيوز / ٧- أوثوريتـي /٨- إم بريزن / ٩- أونست /١٠- تل ذا

تروث /١١- رس بكت ١٢- تل لايز

/ ١٣ - فري د م أُق إكس بريشـن / ١٤- إك سـيد

١٥- تـور تـشا رد .

* Language لـغـة :

1- The reporter gives people an analysis of some events, thus
    affecting their reactions.

إن المراسل يعطي الناس تحليلاً لبعض الأحداث وهو بذلك يؤثر في ردور أفعالهم.

↓ يأتي بعدها فعل رابع يعبر عن الناتج عن الجملة السابقة

(thus ولهذا -وبذلك)

X

2- We respect **reporters** . <u>Reporters</u> give us facts.

↓

We respect reporters who give us facts.
We hate reporters who hide facts from people.

إننا نكره المراسلين الذين يُخفون الحقائق عن الناس .

3- We **expect** reporters to report events frankly.

↓

يتوقع من (بدون حرف جر)

إننا نتوقع من المراسلين أن ينقلوا الأحداث بصراحة .

4- It is wrong to **hide** facts **from** people .

من الخطأ أن نُخفي الحقائق عن الناس.

5- We are **aware of** this fact. إننا على وعي بهذه الحقيقة .

* **Fill in the spaces with suitable words :**

1- The reporter is .... an important job.

2- He provides people with information about

.... that take place somewhere.

3- The reporter gives people an .... of an important

event, so he can affect their ....

4- This job is dangerous because the reporter may have to travel to

a ...., where he may .... his life.

5- Sometimes , the reporter's........................ may displease قد تغضب

the authority . In this case , the authority will send him to prison

السـجن , where he is detained and

....

6- I am angry . Your views do not .... me.

7- Honest reporters have problems with the authority because the

later does not allow them .... of expression .

8- If reporters do their job honestly بشرف , they will serve t

.... of ....

9- People need .... reporters who report events

frankly.

10- Some countries .... and ....

reporters who have anti- government ideas .

11- It is important to .... reporters to give people

facts.

12- It is wrong to .... facts from people.

13- We should realize that freedom has ....

14- A good reporter does not .... his limits.

15- The reporter's job is not to .... others.

Composition 58 / Rumours الإشاعات
Write a composition about " rumours ."

I want to tell you about the danger of rumours . Nobody can deny that rumours are bad and dangerous. Rumours are not facts . Rumours are lies. Weak people spread rumours to confuse others. Rumours are dangerous because they hurt people a lot . Rumours are bad because they damage the country's stability. Rumours are bad because they destroy the friendly relations with people. Rumours destroy stability to create confusion. Rumours damage love to plant suspicions and hatred. Rumours are dirty because they are meant to defame others to realize dirty ends.

Rumours are bad news . When you spread a rumour , you spread a lie. You spread destruction. Rumours are a serious problem , so we should fight them. I advise people to ignore people who spread rumours. It is wrong to believe rumour-mongers. If we believe them , we will lose a lot .

In short , rumours are dangerous , so we fight them to avoid disasters . If a rumour- monger tells you something , you should act wisely. Any rash action will result in a disaster.

* Key words :

rumour (1) إشاعة / rumour – monger مروج إشاعات / lies(2) أكاذيب / weak ضعيف / result in يـؤدي إلى / rash action تصرف متهـور / confuse (4) يربك -يشوش على / hurt (3) يؤذي / spread ينتشر -ينشر / stability (6) / confusion (5) تشويش-ارتباك / destroy يدمر / are meant to يُقصـد منهـا / dirty قذرة / spoil تفسد استقرار / plant يزرع / علاقات ودية friendly relations (7) تشوه سمعة defame / avoid يتجنب / يتلف -يخرب damage / يخلق create / ignore يتجاهل hatred (9) الكراهية / suspicion (8) الشك / destruction (10) الدمار / disaster (11) / believe يصدّق / مشكلة خطيرة a serious problem / كارثة / act wisely نتصرف بـحكمـة

ملاحظة نطق : ١- روما رّ/ ٢- لايـز / ٣- هـيـرت / ٤- كن فيوز / ٥- كن فيوجن   ٦ - ستا بـي ليـتي / ٧ - فرندلي ريليشـن / ٨- ساس بيشـن / ٩- هيتـرد / ١٠ - دست رکشن / ١١- دي زاس تار.

● **Fill in the spaces with suitable words :**

1- .... are unreliable news أخبار غير موثوقة .

2- When you .... rumours , you spread ....

3- Some weak people spread rumours to .... others.

4- Rumours are bad because they damage the country's ....

5- Rumours spoil friendly .... with people.

6- Rumours destroy stability to plant ....

7- Rumours plant .... and hatred.

8- When you spread a .... , you spread a lie.

9- When you spread rumours , you spread ....

132

10- Rumours are a .... problem , so we should

.............................them..

* **Re-order these words to make sentences :**

1- wrong / rumour- mongers / believe / is / to / It /

....

2- is / to / rumours / spread / ugly قبيح / It /

....

3- rumour-mongers / avoid / lies / because / We / they / should / spread /

....

4- fight / because / should / destruction / We / bring / rumours / they /

....

5- people / ignore / should / spread / who / rumours / We /

....

6- you / you / spread/ defame / mean to / When/ somebody / a rumour /

....

7- both / is / and / shameful / unfair / It / others / to defame /

....

Composition 59 / Jobs الوظــائـف

● **Write a composition about why jobs are important.**

I want to tell you why jobs are important . Nobody can deny that we benefit a lot from jobs. It is important to do a job . Everybody must have a job. If you have a job , you can live well. But if you don't have a job , you will suffer a lot. It is difficult to live without a job. The job is a means of earning bread. You get a salary for doing a job. You need this salary to meet your daily needs. We respect people who have jobs. We do not respect lazy people who refuse to do a job.

Some people do great jobs because they relieve others a lot . Pilots, teachers, bakers , builders , drivers , policemen and soldiers serve others a lot ; they make life easy and comfortable. We respect these people because they work hard to make life easy for us. In fact , they are struggling to relieve others.

Some people don't have jobs . These people are unemployed . They are jobless people. The worrying thing is the rise in the number of jobless people . Unemployment is   a serious problem . The government should act quickly to solve it lest it should lead to more serious problems. These jobless people may endanger the country's stability .

In short , it is necessary for everybody to have a job , but it is wrong to ignore jobless people.

● **Key words :**

benefit يستفيد / deny ينكر / means وسيلة
ear يكسب / bread قوت / salary راتب
serve يخدم / lazy كسول / respect نحترم
meet your daily needs تلبي حاجاتك اليومية / refuse يرفض
soldiers (1) الجنود / relieve يخفف من معاناة / make يجعل
comfortable (2) مريحة / worrying مقلق / solve تحل
the rise in الإرتفاع في / serious خطيرة

the number of jobless people عدد الناس العاطلين   act
stability (4)   الحكومة government (3) / تتصرف
ignore   lest خشية أن / تؤدي إلى lead to / استقرار
unemployed عاطل عن العمل   يعرّض للخطر endanger / يتجاهل
unemployment (5) البطالة /
struggle (6) يناضلون - يكافحون

....

* ملاحظة نطـق : ١- سول جرز / ٢- كام فارتابل / ٣- قا فـر مـنـت
٤- ستا بيليتي / ٥- أن إمبلوي مـنـت / ٦- سـترا قـل

* **Fill in the spaces with suitable words :**

1-Nobody can deny that jobs are ....
2-We .... a lot from jobs. We need a job to

....

134

3- If you .... a job , you can live well.

4- If you do not have a job , you will .... a lot.

5- If you do a good job , you will get a good ....

6- The job is a means of .... bread.

7- We need to get a salary to .... our daily
needs.

8- Some people do great jobs that make life ....
for us.

9- Farmers and policemen work hard to make ....
easy and ....

10- We .... people who serve us.

11- .... is a serious problem , so we should
solve it.

Composition 60 / A hurricane   إعـصـار

● **Write a composition about a hurricane (an earthquake زلزال ,   a war)
that hit a town in your country.**

   I want to tell you about a hurricane that hit a town in the north of
my country causing a lot of damage . The hurricane hit the town in the
early morning when most people were asleep. The hurricane destroyed
everything. It destroyed hundreds of houses , thus making thousands of
people homeless. The hurricane destroyed roads , thus making traffic
difficult. The hurricane destroyed the airport , thus cutting off the town
from the outside world. The hurricane flooded coastal areas , thus killing a
big number of people .   Thousands of trees were pulled and water pipes
damaged. People suffered from water and food shortages

In fact , the hurricane changed the face of the town . If you come to the area , you will see destruction everywhere.

This is a serious situation. We should do something to relieve the homeless. We should send urgent aid. We should send tents , food and medicine. We should act quickly to avoid a disaster. If we act quickly , we will save many lives. If we do nothing , a disaster will inevitably take place.

● **Key words :**

hurricane (1) اعصار / hit ضرب / north شمال
in the early morning في الصباح الباكر / most معظم
asleep نائمون / destroyed دمر hundreds
مئات (2) / thus وهو بهذا make يجعل /
thousands (3) ألاف homeless مشردون / traffic حركة المرور
airport المطار / cut off عزل
the outside world العالم الخارجي / changed غيّر face وجه
/ area المنطقة
destruction (4) الدمار / a serious situation (5) وضع خطير
relieve نخفف من معاناة / send نرسل / urgent (6) عاجل aid
معونة / tents خيام / medicine دواء act
disaster لكي نتجنب كارثة / inevitably حتـمـاً quickly بسرعة / to avoid a

....

ملاحظة نطق: ١- هاريكن / ٢- ها نـد رد ز / ٣- ثاوزنـدس / ٤- دست ركشن /
٥- أسيرياص ست يو ويشن / ٦- إرجانت / ٧- إن
إيـفـا تـا بــلي

* **Fill in the spaces with suitable words :**

1- A ....hit a town in the north of my country ,
.... a lot of damage. الكثير من الدمار

2- The hurricane ....homes , (thus)
making many people ....

3- The hurricane destroyed the roads , making .... impossible.

4- The hurricane destroyed the airport , thus ....the town from the outside world.

136

5-   The hurricane ....the face of the town.

6-   The hurricane .... the coastal areas.

7-   We should send .... aid to .... the homeless.

8-   We should act .... to avoid a ....

9-   We should send ...., food and ....

10- If we do not act quickly , a human .... will take place.

* **Language لـغـة :**

1- The hurricane hit the town , **causing** a lot of damage.

$$\downarrow$$

(محدثاً - مسبباً) فعل شكل رابع يعبر عما نتج عن الفعل الذي سبقه.

2- The hurricane hit the town, **thus وهو بذلك** causing a lot of
   damage .

* المعنى في الجملتين واحد . إن الإعصار ضرب المدينة محدثاً الكثير من الدمار

3- The hurricane destroyed homes , (thus) making many
     people homeless.

4- An earthquake flattened many houses, thus killing hundreds
     of people.

إن زلـزالاً سـوى الـكـثيــر من الـبـيـوت بالأرض وهو بهـذا قـتـل مئـا ت من الـنـاس .

Composition 61 / A celebration احـتـفـال

* **Write a composition about a celebration in your country.**

I want to tell you about a celebration in my country. Muslims

fast in Ramadan . At the end of this month, people have a four-day holiday to

celebrate Eid- Al –Fitr. They celebrate this event to mark the end of fasting

and to show their joy that they have fasted to please Allah. The people celebrate this Eid in different ways. They wear new clothes and go out to pray in the open air at sun-rise . Then , they visit relatives and friends to exchange wishes of a happy Eid. People make cakes and give children money. In the evening , they start fireworks and popular dances. They do that to show their pleasure. Rich people share poor people the joy of the Eid. This joy-sharing is characteristic of this Eid.

I feel happy because all people are happy. I like this celebration because people gather to celebrate an important event.

* **Key words :**

celebrate (1) يحتفل بـ / celebration احتفال / fast يصوم

in different ways بطرق مختلفة / wear يلبس / pray يصلي

new clothes ملابس جديدة / in the open air في الهواء الطلق

at sun-rise عند شروق الشمس / relatives (2) أقارب

exchange (3) يتبادل / wish أمنية / wishes أمنيات-تمنيات

fireworks ألعاب نارية / popular dances (4) رقصات شعبيةshow

pleasureمـنـاسـبـة event / joy فرحة / يُظهر

pleasure (5) فرحة -سعادة / فرحة -سعادة (5)

138

joy- sharing المشاركة في الفرح

characteristic of (6) مميز لـ - ميزة لـ

gather (7) يتجمعون

....

* ملاحظة نـطـق : ١- سيـليـب ريت / ٢- ريــلا تـثـز / ٣- إكس تـشـينج

٤- بوب يولار دان سيـز / ٥- بليجار

٦- كاراك تار إستك أق / ٧- قاا ذ ار

Composition 62 / My opinion of celebrations   رأيـي في الإحـتـفـالات

* Write a composition expressing your opinion of
celebrations .Are you for or against them ?

I want to tell you my opinion of celebrations . I am for the idea
because people benefit a lot from celebrations. Nobody can deny
the advantages. First , we celebrate important events that are
part of our heritage. We celebrate to remember our heritage .
Celebrations are a means of maintaining heritage. To maintain
heritage means maintaining the country's sovereignty . Second ,
people gather to show the world their national character and unity.
Celebrations bring people together so that social

cohesion becomes a reality. Third , our children learn good things from these celebrations. Fourth , celebrations serve our economy because people spend a lot of money . Fifth , when people gather to celebrate an important event , they put aside their differences . Real reconciliations take place during a celebration. .

But celebrations have got some disadvantages. People spend too much money on them , which spoils the real meaning of a celebration. I am against this waste of money . Another thing, some reckless people use fire-arms which endanger others .

In short , it is good to celebrate important events , but we should do that in a reasonable way. It is not to wrong to celebrate important events , but it is wrong to do that at the expense of our morals. People should remember that they should use noble means to realize noble goals.

* Key words :

pinion رأي / celebrate يحتفل بـ / celebration (1) احتفال
for مؤيد / against ضد / event مناسبة
part of جزء من / heritage (2) تراث / remember (3) نتذكر
protect نحمي / culture (4) ثقافة / gather يتجمعون
to show the world لكي يُظهرون للعالم / a means وسيلة
their national character (5) شخصيتهم الوطنية unity
(6) الوحدة / serve تخدم / reckless طائش
fire-arms أسلحة نارية / economy (7) اقتصاد
endanger يعَرض للخطر / spend ينفق spoil
يُفسد / the real meaning المعنى الحقيقي / during أثناء

....

* ملاحظة نطق : ١- سيليب ريشن / ٢- هيريتج / ٣- ري ممبر / ٤-
٥- ذيـر نـا شـو نال كـا راك تا(ر) / كـال تـشا(ر) /
٦- يـونـيـتي / ٧- اكـو نـومي
a waste of money تبديد المال / realize يحقق
in a reasonable way (1) بطريقة معقولة
advantages مزايا / disadvantage عيب social
cohesion (2) تماسك اجتماعي / a reality (3) أمر واقع

bring ... together تجمَع سـويـاً   /   maintain (4) يصون

at the expense of .... على حسـاب /

noble means وسائل نبـيـلة /

reconciliation (5) مصـالحة   /   sovereignty (6) سـيـادة - اسـتقلال

....

Fill in the spaces with suitable words :

1- I am .... celebrations because we benefit a lot from them.

2- Nobody can .... the advantages.

3- We .... important events. These events are
    .... our heritage.

4- It is important to .... our heritage.

5- Celebrations are a means of ....
    our heritage.

6 We want to show the world our national ....

7- Celebrations serve the .... of the country

8- People .... a lot of money on celebrations.

9- It is wrong to spend too much money on ....
    because this will .... the real meaning of a celebration.

Composition 63 / Cultural festivals المـهـرجانـات الثـقـافيـة

• **Write a composition saying what you think of cultural festivals. Are you for or against them ?**

    I want to express my opinion of cultural festivals. Nobody can
deny that cultural festivals are useful. They appeal to me a lot because
we benefit a lot from them. The advantages are great. First , these festivals
give people access to other cultures. This will enrich our culture. Thanks to
modern technology , the world has become too small and things are
changing rapidly. This makes it necessary to see other cultures. Second ,
people will learn many good things from these festivals ; they learn to
choose what is good for them. Third, thanks to these festivals , we can
keep in touch

with other people so that we can exchange ideas with others. Fourth ,
cultural festivals can promote noble things like peace , freedom and
tolerance among the world's peoples . The face-to-face gathering will
create a common culture of understanding and fruitful dialogue.

In short , we need cultural festivals to show that
different cultures can co-exist peacefully. We should
make sure that cultural festivals realize this noble goal.
It is not wrong to have cultural festivals , but it is wrong to
do that at the expense of our morals .

● **Key words :**

cultural festivals (1) المهرجانات الثقافية / appeal to تروق لـ
benefit نستفيد / advantages المزايا
give people access to تيسّر للناس الوصول إلى / culture (2) ثقافة enrich (3)
التـقنية technology (4) / بفضل thanks to / تثري
become أصبح / change تتغير / rapidly (5) بسرعةchoose (6)
/ exchange يتباد لون / يختـارون
with others مع الأخرين
face – to – face المباشر -وجهاً لوجه / gathering اللقاء –التجمع
co-exist (7) تتعا يـش / fruitful مثـمـر
peacefully (8) بطريقـة سلمية / promote يـروج لـ tolerance
التفاهم understanding / التـسامح
dialogue (9) الحوار / create يخـلـق
keep in touch with نبقى على صلة مع
at the expense of على حساب / morals الأخـلاق

....

ملاحظة نطق: ١- كال تشارال فيستي ڤا لز / ٢- كال تشار / ٣- إن رتـش / ٤ - تك
نولوجي / ٥ - رابدلي / ٦- تـشـوز / ٧- كو إقزسست / ٨ - بيس فولي / ٩-
دايا لوق

* **Fill in the spaces with suitable words :**

1- Cultural .... are useful . Nobody can deny the .

....

2- I am for the cultural festivals ; they .... to
me a lot.

142

3- We need cultural festivals to see other ....

4- We need cultural festivals to .... other people our original culture.

5- If we see other cultures , we will .... our culture.

6- The world is .... rapidly thanks to modern technlology.

7- The world has ....too small thanks to modern technology.

8- It is necessary to see other ....

9- People .... many useful things from these festivals.

10- Cultural festivals are a means of .... freedom , understanding and ....

Composition 64 / Radioactivity
الـــنـــشـــاط الإشـــعـــاعـــي

- **Write a composition about radioactivity.**

I want to shed light on radioactivity. Some materials are radioactive . A material has millions of atoms. Each atom has a nucleus. Radioactivity takes place in the nucleus of the atom. When the nucleus is split , energy in the form of radiation is released. This radioactivity is useful in many ways . First , we can use it to find the age of dead animals and plants. Doctors are using it to know when a person died. Second , we can use radiation to preserve food. The process is called irradiation , which means that radiations are given to some foods to kill the bacteria in them . Finally , we can use radioactivity to generate huge amounts of electricity. In this way , we can solve our energy problems .

But radioactivity is harmful for people. It can hurt people a lot ; it can cause blindness. Radioactivity can kill people too . This is a big problem , so scientists are working hard to solve it. We can say that radioactivity has advantages and disadvantages. We should try to reduce the disadvantages .

In short , radioactivity is a source of cheap , renewable energy , but we should take care that it does not cause people problems. People need risk-free energy . Scientists should do their best to realize this goal.

* Key words :

radiate يشع- / radiation إشعاع - إنبعاث الإشعاع

(1) radioactivity النشاط الإشعاعي / radioactive مشّع / dead ميت

(3) nucleus نواة / atom ذرة / material (2)

energy الطاقة / split ينشطر- يشطر / يتم- يحدث take place

animals الحيوانات / release يحرر / على هيئة in the form of

is عملية (5) process / يحفظ preserve (4) / ضار harmful

called تسمى / irradiation إكساب الشيء إشعاعاً

(7) can cause يمكن أن يسبب / يحل solve / يؤذي hurt (6)

(9) scientist العالم / العمى blindness (8)

مزايا advantages / نحاول try / يعملون بجدٍ working hard

مصدر source / يقلل من reduce / عيوب disadvantages

144

renewable متجدد / take care نحذر / cause يسبب

risk-free خال من المخاطر / do their best يبذلوا قصارى جهودهم

....

ملاحظة نطق : 1- ريد يو أكتڤيتي / 2- ما تيريال / 3- نيو ك

لياص   4- بريزيرڤ / 5- برو سس / 6- هيرت / 7- كان

كوز   8- بلايند نس / 9- سا يا ن تست

Composition 65 / The Palestinians' struggle
نضال الفلسطينيين

The Palestinians had their homeland usurped in 1948 and millions of them have been living in miserable refugee camps in neighbouring Arab countries. The Israelis have set up their own state ignoring the Palestinian rights. The Palestinians insist on restoring their own homeland by all means. They are not ready to concede the right of return and the right of having a fully sovereign state with Jerusalem as a capital.

The Palestinians have the full right to resist and fight the invaders.
They are fighting to restore their country which the Israelis usurped in
1948.The Palestinians want freedom and independence. The Palestinians are
ready to negotiate   a compromise , but the Israelis
deny the Palestinian rights , supported by some Big Powers and some regional
powers. The Israelis are killing people and destroying everything . The Israelis
are using force to silence the Palestinians , but the Palestinian will-power is
stronger than the Israeli tanks and shells.

The Palestinans are aware of the current world situation which sides
with the Zionist invaders . But they will never recognize the Isreali state so
long as their rights are ignored by the Zionist usurpers . The Palestinians are
victims of the Isreali terrorism , so they cannot recognize the legitimacy of
usurpation.

The Palestinians are fighting alone suffering heavy losses. The
Arabs and Muslims are keeping silent. This is shameful . The Israeli crimes
must stop. Arabs and Muslims

should do something to stop the Israeli aggression. If the Arabs ignore this aggression , they will suffer sooner or later at the hand of the Israelis. The Israelis dream of having a Jewish state extending from The River Nile to The Euphrates.

The Palestinians want to communicate this message to the world : peace will never prevail unless the legitimate Palestinian rights are fulfilled . The Palestinians are aware of the big challenges facing their struggle , but they have the will and the right. The Palestinians derive their might from their right and from the relentless will to regain this right

- **Key words :**

usurped (1) اغتُصب / miserable (2) بائسة – تعيسة

refugee camps (3) معسكرات للاجئين

neighbouring (4) مجاورة

set up أنشئوا / ignore يتجاهل

rights الحقوق / insist on (5) يصر على restore

homeland الوطن / يسترد – يسترجع

the بأي ثمن – مهما كلف الأمر / concede (6) يتنازل عن by all means

right of return (7) حق العودة / sovereign (8) ذات سيادة

resist (9) يقاوم / invaders (10) الغزاة

independence (11) الإستقلال / negotiate (12) يتفاوض على

compromise (13) حل وسط / silence يسكت

واعون بـ / aware of   قوة إرادة   will- power

recognize يقـف إلى جانب / side with   الـوضع الـحالي   current situation (14)

طـالما / so long as   يعترف بـ   (15)

صهيوني (17) Zionist /   المغتصبون   usurpers (16)

ضحايا (19) victims /   ما لم   unless (18)

السلام peace /   قضية   cause

shameful خسائر فادحة (20) heavy losses /   يعانون – يتكبدون   suffer

الـعدوان (22) aggression الـجرائم / crimes (21)   مـخزي

تمتد extend /

legitimate (25) يـوصل communicate (24) /   نـهـر الفرات   The Euphrates (23)

يوفي بـ fufill /   مشروعة

struggle (28) التحديات challenges (27) /   شرعية – مشروعية   legitimacy (26)

يستمد derive (29)   اغتصاب usurpation (31) /   نضال

لا تـلين – صلبة relentless (30)   قوة   might /

قذائـف / shells

---

* مـلاحظة نـطـق : ١- يـو زير بد /٢- ميـز رابـل / ٣- ريف يوجي كامبس / ٤ -

نيبا رنق / ٥- إنـسـست / ٦- كـون سيـد / ٧- ري تيـرن / ٨- سـاڤـرن /

٩- ري زيـسـت / ١٠- إن ڤـيدا ارز / ١١- إندي بـن د نس / ١٢-

نيقو شيـيت/ ١٣ - كـومبرو مـا يـز

١٤- كـا رنت ست يـو ويـشـن / ١٥- ريـكـوق نـا يـز /

١٦- يـوز يـر بـارز / ١٧- زايـو نـسـت /١٨- أن لـس / ١٩- ڤـك تـمز

٢٠- هـيـڤـي لـوسـيـز / ٢١- كـرايـمـز / ٢٢- أ قـر يـشـن

148

٢٣- ذا أيو فريتس / ٢٤- كوم يو نيكيت
ليجي تيمت
٢٦- ليجي تما سي / ٢٧- تشا لنجز / ٢٨- ستراقل
٢٩- دي رايڤ / ٣٠- ري لنت لس / ٣١- يوز ير بيشن

Composition 66 / Ramadan : the month of the fast .
* Write a composition about the fast .

Islam has five pillars : the belief in Allah , the belief that Muhammad
is Allah's Prophet , prayer , Zakat , the fast and the Haj . Ramadan is the
month in which Muslims fast from dawn to sun-set. Allah commands Muslims
to fast , and Muslims must obey the order. Allah commands Muslims to do
things that do them good. We learn many good things from fast. First , when
you fast , your stomach takes rest. It is wrong to keep filling your stomach with
food. Second , when you fast, you get hungry . Then you remember the
hungry and poor people. Third , all Muslims are the same ; every able
Muslim

must fast . Only ill and weak people are excepted . Fourth , when you fast , you learn to control yourself. Fifth , Muslims come to realize that life is not always easy.　A Muslim has to face hard times to learn patience and endurance. Sixth, people are closer in Ramadan to Allah than they are in other months.

We receive Ramadan with a promise that we will remain close to Allah. We learn many good things ; we learn piety , which means that you distance yourself from bad things so that you will please Allah whose greatest reward is Paradise .

● **Key words :**

pillars أركان	belief الإيمان /
Prophet (1) نبي	prayer الصلاة /
fast يصوم - الصوم	command يأمـر /
obey يطيـع	order الأمـر /
stomach (2) المعدة	take rest ترتاح /
weak ضعيف	except (3) يسـتـثـنى / control
يتحكم في	patience (4) الصبر /
please يــرضـي	endurance (5) القدرة على التحمل/
promise (6) الوعد	remain close to يظل قريباً من/ piety (7)
التقوى distance/ ينأ بـ	
reward مكافأة	Paradise (8) الجنة /

....

150

ملاحظة نطق : ١- بـرو فـت / ٢- سـتوماك / ٣- إك سبـت / ٤- بيـش يـانص

٥- إند يو رانص / ٦- بـرو مس / ٧- باياتي / ٨- بارا دايز

Composition 67 / A true friend   الـصديـق الـحق

Write a composition about this topic : " A friend in need is   a friend indeed."   الصديق في وقت الضيق هو الصديق حقاً.

I would like to write about true friends. Nobody can deny that we need friends a lot. It is impossible to live alone. You need a friend to talk to . Nobody can deny the advantages of having a friend. First , you need a friend to help you solve your problems. When you are in trouble , you appeal to a friend for help. The true friend will not betray you. He will act quickly to relieve you. Second, you need a friend when you have to decide something. You are worried and confused because you cannot make a decision. A true friend will show you how to act decisively. Third , you need a friend to share you your sorrow. You feel sad because you lose a dear person. The true friend will do his best to help you overcome your sorrow. Fourth, you need a friend to share you your joys. You have joyful moments . Unless you have true friends , you will not fully enjoy these joyful moments. Fifth, you need a friend to exchange ideas with him and to disclose your secrets to him.

What kind of friends do we need ? You need true friends who do not betray you when you need them. I advise you to make friends with good people . If you mix with good friends , you will benefit a lot. You will learn many good things from them. If you mix with bad people , they will destroy you. It is useful to make friends , but you have to take care. You have to choose your friends carefully. Bad friends can bring you a disaster.

In short , we need true friends who come to relieve us when we need them. It is useful to make friends , but it is wrong to make friends with bad people .

* Key words :

in trouble (1) في ورطة	appeal to تناشد /
betray يخون - يخذ ل	confused مضطرب /
decision (2) قرار	decisively بشكل حاسم /
share يشاطر	sorrow (3) حزن /
overcome يتغلب على	disclose تفشي /
secrets (4) أسرار	destroy يدمر /
disaster (5) كارثه	relieve يخفف من معاناة /
take care يأخذ الحذر	

----

* ملاحظة نطق : ١- إن ترابـل / ٢- دي سيجن / ٣- سورو /
٤- سـيك ريتـس / ٥- ديـزاس تـار

153

Composition 68 / Sports festivals

المـهـرجانات الـرياضية

* Write a composition about sports events.

I want to tell you about sports events . Nobody can deny that sports events are important. We need these events because we will benefit a lot from them. Nobody can deny the advantages. First, sport events encourage sportsmen to mix with others , so they will improve their performance . Second , sports events encourage sports tourism . Sports fans come to a country in great numbers and spend lots of money . This will improve the economy of the country. Third , thanks to these sport events , the host country becomes famous all over the world because the TV stations broadcast these events worldwide. Countries use these sports events to promote their cultures. Fourth , the host country will have to build more sports facilities . The host country will have to develop its sports facilities . Fifth , sports events bring people closer , thus promoting noble values like friendship , understanding and co-operation .

In short , sports events are useful because they promote fair competition . We need fair play . We should use these sports events to realize this noble goal. It is true that we spend lots of money on sports events , but the advantages are great.

sports events	مناسبات رياضية /	encourage (1)	يشجع
sportsmen	الرياضيون /	mix with	يختلط مع
improve	يحسُن /	performance (2)	أداء
sports fans	أنصار الرياضة /	in great numbers	بأعداد كبيرة
economy	اقتصاد /	the host country	البلد المضيف
broadcast	تبث /	promote	يروج لـ
culture (3)	ثقافة /	facilities (4)	منشآت
develop	يطور /	bring .... closer	تقرُب
values (5)	قيم /	co-operation (6)	التعاون
fair competition	منافسة عادلة /	advantages (7)	المزايا
friendship (8)	الصداقة		

ملاحظة نطــق : ١- إن كا ريج / ٢- بارفور ما نـس / ٣- كـل تـشار /
٤ - فاسـيـلي تـيـز ٥ - ثّـا ل يوز / ٦- كـو أوبـي ريشـن

٧- أدڤا نتـيـجز /٨- فرند شب

155

Composition 69 / Asking for changes المطالبة بالتغيير

* **Write a composition about this topic :**

" Recommending changes to your town."

I want to tell you about changes that people need to see in their town. I am sorry to complain about some problems in our town. I want to suggest what we should do to solve these problems.

We have many problems in our town. First , some houses are too old. Why not restore some of them? Why don't we remove the others ? Second , some roads are too narrow , thus causing accidents. I suggest that we should improve them. Third, we see too many traffic jams that make traffic too difficult. We could replace the roundabouts with traffic- lights. Fourth, we see too much rubbish everywhere. That is ugly. Why not place containers everywhere ? Why not increase the number of cleaners? Fifth, some factories and workshops are too close to houses , thus causing too much pollution and too much noise. People don't accept that. Why not move them to the industrial area? Sixth , we see too few green areas. People need green areas a lot. Why not plant trees and grass everywhere ?

In short , we suffer a lot from these problems. I think that we should act quickly to relieve people. I hope that these problems will disappear soon. People hope that they will see real changes soon. We hope that our town will change for the better soon.

* **Key words :**

complain يشتكي	/ suggest (1) يقترح	/ restore نرمم - نجدد
remove يزيل	/ narrow ضيق	/ improve يحسّن
traffic jams اختناقات مرورية	/ replace يستبدل	
ugly (2) قبيح	/ place نضع	/ container حاوية
increase نزيد من	/ the number of cleaners عدد عمال النظافة	
factory مصنع	/ factories مصانع	/ workshop ورشة

156

إزعاج - ضوضاء noise / تلوث pollution (4) / تسبب cause (3)

move ننقل / industrial (5) area منطقة صناعية

plant نزرع / suffer from يعاني من / act نتصرف

relieve نخفف من معاناة / disappear تختفي

----

* ملاحظة نطق: ١- ساجست / ٢- أقلي / ٣- كوز / ٤- بولوشن /

٥- اند ست ريال /

* **Complete these sentences :**

1- We .... a lot from many problems in our town.

2- I suggest that we should .... these problems to relieve people.

3- We have too many traffic jams which .... traffic too difficult.

4- Why not .... the roundabouts ? We could .... traffic-lights instead of them. If we do that , traffic jams will ....

5- We see too much rubbish. We could .... this problem by .... the number of cleaners.

6- Some factories are too .... to houses , thus .... too much .... and too much noise. Why not .... these factories to the .... area ?

7- We see too many stray dogs and cats which .... **public health.** الصحة العامة

8- People need some green areas , where they can ....

9- Some roads are too narrow , thus .... accidents.

10- Some people smoke in public places. **Why not pass a law that forbids smoking ?**

لما ذا لا نجيـز قـانـونـاً يـحـرّم التدخين ؟

157

Compostion 70 /   Two TV programmes.

* **Write a composition about two TV programmes you
  lately watched.**

      I would like to tell you about two TV programmes I watched. I want to say that I did not like them at all. They were bad because they were full of sex and violence. We do not accept this kind of programmes.

      The first film was full of shameful scenes that offend decent people. We do not need sex films that spoil our young people. We need useful ones. The other film was full of violence. I am not against showing violence on TV , but I am against showing too much of it . It is wrong to show too much violence on TV because our children may learn to be violent. Showing too much violence on TV might mislead children into committing similar acts.

      These programmes are harmful , so we should stop them . We should have programmes that amuse and teach people good things. We expect the TV station to show programmes that respect the morals of people. I hope that this problem will disappear soon.

      In short , people suffer a lot from bad programmes , so we should relieve them by giving them useful , interesting programmes. We should give people programmes that they need. We are for useful programmes , but we are against bad ones. TV stations should realize this fact and act quickly to put an end to this serious problem. It is not wrong to show people programmes , but it is wrong to do that at the expense of our morals.

● **Key words :**

عنيف violent / العنف (1) violence / الجنس sex
offend / scenes (3) مناظر-مشاهد / مخزي (2) shameful
harmful / يعرض show / مهذب decent / تسئ إلى
ضارة (4) / expect يتوقع من / amuse (5) تبسط – تمتع
teach تعلّم / respect يحترم / morals (6) أخلاقيات
يضلل (7) mislead

يتصرف act / يرتكب أعمالاً متماثلة (8) commit similar acts
يضع حداً لـ put an end to / يدرك realize
على حساب at the expense of

----

* ملاحظة نطق : ١- ڤا يولنس / ٢- شيم فل / ٣- سينز / ٤- هارم فل / ٥- أم
يوز / ٦- مورا لز / ٧- مس ليد / ٨- كومت سيمي لار أكتس /

* **Complete these sentences :**

1- I want to complain أشتكي about a film I .... last
   night. It was full of .... scenes.

2- We do not .... this kind of films.

3- People do not need .... films . People need ....
   films.

4- We need films that .... people good things.

5- We need films that .... the morals of people.

6- Some films are .... , so we should fight them.

7- We should fight films that .... young people.

8- The other film was .... violence scenes.

9- It is wrong to .... too much violence on TV.
   This has a negative effect on our ....
   They might .... similar acts .

10- It is not wrong to .... people many programmes,
    but we should take care that these programmes do not
    .... the morals of people.

159

Composition 71 / The two-day weekend الإجازة الإسبوعية

* **Write a composition about " A two-day weekend ."**

I want to tell you my opinion of the two-day weekend. I am for it because we will benefit a lot from it. Nobody can deny the advantages. First , a two-day weekend means more time to relax. It is useful to relax after five working days. If we relax , we will be more productive . If we relax , we will come back to school full of energy. Second , thanks to the two-day weekend , we will have more time to practise our hobbies. Third , if we have a two-day weekend , we can study and revise on our own. Fourth , the two-day weekend has made the school work a great pleasure. The school work is no longer boring, It has become interesting.

In short , the two-day weekend is a good idea and I expect people to benefit from it. People need real fun. They should use this weekend well to realize this goal. I hope that people will take this weekend seriously. It is good to have a two-day weekend , but the way you spend it is more important.

● **Key words :**

for مؤيد / benefit نستفيد / advantages المزايا
productive (1) منتج / practise (2) يمارس / hobby هواية
hobbies هوايات / revise نراجع / on our own بمفردنا
a great pleasure متعة كبيرة / boring ممل
no longer لم يعد / lose يخسر / expect يتوقع من
real fun متعة حقيقية / realize this goal يحقق هذا الهدف
take .... seriously (3) يأخذ .. مأخذ الجد
has made قد جعلت

* ملاحظة --

نطق : ١- برو دك تيـڤ / ٢- براك تـس / ٣- سيـر ياص لي

160

Composition 72 / Learning foreign languages

تعـــلـــم

لــغـــات أجـنـبـيــة

* Write a composition about : " Learning two foreign languages by high school students."

I want to tell you my opinion of high school students learning two foreign languages. I think it is a great idea because it will benefit many students. Nobody can deny the advantages. First , the world has become a small village thanks to modern technology. This makes it necessary for people to know more languages. We need more languages so that we can communicate with other people from other countries. Second , if you know more languages, you can easily continue with your education abroad. Third , languages give you access to more cultures. If you know more languages, you can mix with many people . You can also make more friends , so you can develop your way of thinking. Fourth , it is easy to learn foreign languages when you are young. Finally , we learn foreign languages to show others that we are free of fanaticism and ready to receive good ideas regardless of their source. A knowledge of foreign languages helps one make use of the Internet , thus making the world of knowledge accessible.

In short , it is good to learn foreign languages , but we should take care that this does not take place at the expense of our mother language . It is useful for our children to learn foreign languages , but it is wrong to do that at the expense of Arabic , the language of the Holy Qur'an.

* Key words :

foreign (1) أجنبي / benefit تفيد- تـنفع / abroad بالخارج
a small village قرية صغيرة / continue (2) تواصل
have access to لديك مدخل على / free of متحرر من / ready مستعد
culture (3) ثقافة / fanaticism (4) التعصب / receive تـتلقى regardless of بغض النظر / source (5) المصدر / take place يتم at the expense of على حساب / accessible (7) سهـل الـمنـال / knowledge (6) الـمعرفة / the mother language اللغـة الأم ---
-----

* ملاحظـة نـطـق : ١- فورين / ٢- كون تنيو / ٣- كا ل تشا ر / ٤- فا نا تي سيزم /
٥ - سورس / ٦- نـا لـدج / ٧- أكـسـيـسي بـول

161

Composition 73 / Tourism السياحة

* **Write a composition about : " Are you for or against tourists coming to your country?"**

I would like to express my opinion of tourists coming to my country. I am for the idea because we benefit a lot from it. The idea appeals to me a lot . I think that we should do everything to encourage tourism . Nobody can ignore the advantages . First , tourists spend a lot of money , which will improve the economy of the country. Second , tourists bring with them new ideas that will enrich our culture. Third , we can show our culture to tourists. In this way , we will remove barriers to the exchange of ideas among the peoples of the world. Fourth , the world has become a small village , so it has become necessary to encourage tourists to come to our country. We need tourists to show them that we are part of the world . Thanks to tourism , we can promote the achievements of our country. I am for this face-to-face gathering because it will benefit everybody. Fifth , Tourism is a means of promoting the values of peace , understanding and freedom.

In short , it is useful to have more tourists coming to our country , so we should do something to attract them . We should provide first-class tourist facilities to realize this goal. Tourism is useful , but we should take care that it does not cause us problems . It is not wrong to have tourists coming to our country , but it is wrong to promote tourism at the expense of our morals.

express يعبّر عن	/	appeal to تروق لـ	
economy اقتصاد	/	bring with them يجلبون معهم	
enrich تثري	/	take care يحتاط	
remove يزيل	/	barriers (1) الحواجـز	
xchange تبادل	/	peoples شعوب	
among بين	/	part جـزء	
goal الهدف	/	It is our duty to (2) من واجبنا	attract
نجذب	/	realize نحقق	
encourage (3) نـشـجـع	/	first-class درجة أولى	
promote يروج لـ	/face-to – face gathering التجمع	
goal الهدف	/values (4) قيم	
provide نوفر	/ tourist facilities منشأ ت سياحيه	
cause us problems ليس عيباً أن	/It is not wrong to تسبب لنا مشاكل	
at the expense of أخلاقنا	/our morals (5) على حساب	

ملاحظـة نـطـق: ١- باريارز / ٢- ديوتي / ٣- إن كـا رج /٤- ڤاليوز / ٥- أوار

مو را لز

Composition 74 / Working women

* **Write a composition about this topic : What you think of women working outside.**

I want to tell you my opinion of women working outside . I am for that because working women benefit a lot from that. Nobody can deny the advantages. First , a working woman will learn many good things; she will learn how to rely on herself.   She will learn how to act on her own.   Second, a working woman has a sense of security and a sense of confidence because she will not remain at mercy of the man . Third , the working woman shares the man the responsibility for the family. Both men and women should work together for the welfare of their children. Fourth , if a woman works , she will improve her way of thinking. Fifth, both men and women should work together to develop the country. Women are   an important part of the community , so it is unfair to ignore them. Women should take part in the development of the country.   Finally , a working woman has a better standard of living than others. Working women can serve the economy of the country. We have seen many successful business-women .

It is good for women to work everywhere , but they must take care . They should do the right jobs lest they should face problems. If they follow this advice , they will benefit a lot. If they ignore this advice , they will suffer a lot. Women are free , but they should use this freedom wisely. If they use freedom well , they can realize their goals easily. If they misuse this freedom , they will lose everything.   Freedom is everyone's goal , but freedom has limits . If we ignore these limits , freedom becomes a disaster. I am for women's freedom of choice , but I am against any misuse of freedom.

rely on يعتمد على / act on her own تتصرف بمفردها share يشاطر
/ a sense of security إحساس بالأمان a sense of confidence إحساس بالثقه
way of thinking طريقة التفكير
lest they should face خشية أن يوجهوا
ignore يتجاهل / remain تبقى at the
mercy of تحت رحمة / successful ناجحات suffer يعاني /
responsibility المسؤلية / limits حدود misuse سوء استخدام - يسيئ استخدام
/ disaster كارثة against ضد / freedom of choice حرية الاختيار
for the welfare من أجل رفاهية / It is
unfair من الظلم أن / take part in يشارك development تنمية
serve يخدم / economy اقتصاد standard of living مستوى
معيشة

* Complete these sentences :

1- I am .... the idea of women .... outside.

2- Nobody can .... the advantages.

3- The woman will .... many good things.

4- She will learn how to .... on her own .

5- The working woman has a .... of security and
a.............................. of ....

6- The woman is .... of the community , so it is
important that she shares the the man the ....
for the children.

7- Men and women belong to ينتمون إلى the same country ,
so both should work .... for the ....
their country.

8- It is good for women to work everywhere , but they should
.... lest they should get into trouble.

Composition 75 / Traffic- jams الإختناقات المرورية

Write a composition about this topic : " Traffic jams are a problem that should come to an end soon."

I want to express my opinion of traffic jams. The traffic situation is getting worse because we have too many traffic-jams today . People suffer a lot from traffic jams because they cause too many problems. Nobody can ignore the fact that traffic jams make traffic unbearable . In the first place , traffic- jams impede traffic , so people cannot move easily from one place to another. Second , when the roads are busy with too many cars , people cannot reach their destinations on time. As a result, traffic-jams waste people's time . Third , traffic-jams cause people psychological tensions ; people become restless when they get trapped. Traffic-jams unnerve drivers. Fourth , traffic-jams may affect badly the engine. Sometimes , cars break down , which worsens traffic a lot.

Traffic-jams are a serious problem , so we should do something to solve it. We can solve this problem if we know what causes traffic-jams. We should act quickly to relieve people. I suggest that roundabouts should be removed and traffic-lights fitted. This will partly solve the problem. Why not change the working hours ? Why don't schools have their own working times ? Civil servants could report for duty at different times. Why do all people have to go to work at one time ? Lorries and big coaches should not be allowed during rush-hours . Narrow roads cause traffic jams. So why not build wide roads ?

In short , traffic-jams are bad , but we can overcome them . People need easy traffic. It is only through implementing my recommendations that we can realize this goal . I do hope that this problem will disappear soon.

● Key words :

traffic-jams اختناقات مروريه / situation (1) الوضع ignore (2) يتجاهل / busy (4) مزدحمة unbearable (3) لا يطاق / impede (5) يعيق In the first place في المقام الأول / destinations (6) الجهات المقصودة reach يصل إلى / restless متبرم psychological tensions (7) اضطرابات نفسيه / تثير أعصاب unnerve (8) ينحصر(يصبح حبيساً) get trapped / beark down تتعطل worsen (9) تؤثر في affect يزيد سوءاً / relieve (10) يخفف من معاناة civil servants موظفون rush-hours (12) ساعات الذروة coaches (11) حافلات / مدنيون through (13) من خلال / overcome يتغلب على / recommendations (15) توصيات implementing (14) تنفيذ

ملاحظة نطق : ١- ست يو ويشن / ٢- إقنور
٣- أن بيرا بل / ٤- بيزي
٥- ام بيد /٦- د ستي نيشنز
٧- سايكو لوجيكال تنشنز
٨- أن نيرڤ / ٩- ويرسن
١٠- ريليڤ / ١١- كوتشز
١٢- رش أوا رز / ١٣- ثرو
١٤- إمبلي منتق
١٥- ريكومند يشنز

167

Composition 76 / The Internet

* **Write a compositon about what you think of the Internet.**

Nobody can deny that the Internet is doing us a great service. The Internet is one of the great achievements . The Internet has come to play a very important part in our life. We need it a lot because we benefit a lot from it. First , you can use the Internet as a source of information ; thanks to the Internet , you can get information about other countries .   Second , you can use the Internet to communicate with others. You can use the Internet to make new friends from other countries . Third, you can use the Internet to improve your English. Fourth , thanks to the Internet , you can exchange ideas with others , so you can develop your way of thinking .

The Internet is useful , so I advise you to use it. If you use it well , you will benefit a lot. We should use the Internet well. It is wrong to misuse the Internet. Some people use the Internet to annoy others , which spoils the real meaning of the Internet. I hope that people will use the Internet to develop their communication skills.

In short , the Internet gives people easy access to the world of knowledge , but we should take care that it does not cause us problems. It is not wrong to use the Internet , but it is wrong to misuse it. If it is misused , it will bring us disasters.

● Key words :

develop يطور / يؤدي لنا خدمة عظيمة do us a great service

skills مهارات الاتصال / achievements (1) انجازات

play a يسبب cause

very important part يلعب دوراً غاية في الأهمية

source (3) مصدر / يتفاهم مع (2) communicate with

communication الاتصال- التواصل

misuse (4) يسيئ استخدام

annoy يضايق / طريقة تفكيرك your way of thinking

spoil يُفسد / يتبادل (5) exchange

take care يأخذ الحذر

the real meaning of المعنى الحقيقي

bring us disasters يجلب لنا كوارث

the world of knowledge (7) عالم المعرفة

give people access to (6) يعطي الناس منفذاً على

....

* ملاحظة نطــق : ١- أتشيئ منتس / ٢- كوم يوني كيت /٣- سورس / ٤-
مس يوز / ٥- إكس تشينج / ٦- أكسيس / ٧- ذا ويرلد أُڤ نا لدج

169

Composition 77 / Town- Planning تخطيط المدن

* Write a composition about town-planning .

    I would like to write about the importance of town-planning. Town-planning means that the town is well- planned so that it makes people proud of it. Nobody can deny the fact that town- planning makes living in a town comfortable. Town-planning has many advantages. First , it ensures that houses and facilities are not haphazardly built so that people can move easily. Second , people have wide roads which make traffic easy and safe. As a result , people don't suffer from traffic- jams or serious car accidents. Third , town-planning ensures safety for people ; it is safe to live in a well-planned town. Accidents rarely happen , and if they happen , it becomes easy to control them. Thanks to excellent town-planning , fire-fighting and rescue operations can run smoothly. In this way , losses can be minimized . Fourth , town-planning ensures that any future expansion can take place , thus avoiding mistakes . Fifth ,town-planning takes into account protection of the environment; it does not allow any transgression of the environment . Thanks to excellent town -planning ,workshops and factories are set up in industrial areas so that people don't suffer from noise or pollution. Finally , town-planning means that people can reach all public facilities easily . Town- planning means easy access to all facilities .

    In short , town-planning makes towns nice places worth living in , but people have a role to play ; they should take care of their towns.

Key words :

town-planning تخطيط المدن / ensure يضمن - يكفل

suffer from يعاني من / haphazardly (1) بطريقة عشوائية

public facilities مرافق عامه / rarely نادراً

عمليات الإنقاذ (2) rescue operations / allow يسمح بـ

take place = happen تحدث - تتم

fire- fighting(3) مكافحة الحرائق / losses الخسائر

a role دور / can be minimized (4) يمكن تقليلها

expansion (5) توسع / avoid يتجنب

mistakes أخطاء run smoothly تعمل بشكل جيد

take into account يضع في الاعتبار protection

حماية / environment (6) البيئة

transgression (7) تجاوز على

industrial areas مناطق صناعية / are set up تقام

pollution تلوث / easy access to سهولة الوصول إلى

worth living in جديرة بأن يعيش فيها المرء

----

* ملاحظة نطق : ١- هاب هازاردلي /٢- رسك يو أبا ريشنز

٣- فاير فاي تنق / ٤- ميني مايزد / ٥- إكس بانشن
٦- إن ڤا يرو منت / ٧- ترانس قريشن

171

Composition 78 / Child labour عـمل الأطفـال
* Write a composition about child labour.

      I want to tell you about child labour . Millions of children are too poor , so they have to work. Poor children cannot go to school because they cannot   pay fees . Many children cannot get education because they are poor. What is worse is the fact that most of these poor children have to do hard jobs . This is unfair . This is wrong. It is shameful that children have to leave school to work for a little money.

      Child labour is a serious problem . We should do something to solve it. Rich people should donate   money to help poor children get education. Governments should not ignore this problem. Every child has the right to get good education. If we don't solve this problem , poor children will have a sense of injustice . If you have a sense of injustice , you will do bad things. If you have a sense of injustice , you will endanger others. Rich people can help by donating money . If they do that , they will save many children . If they help, they will protect the country from crime . I hope that we will act quickly to relieve poor children.

* **Key words :**

وما هـو أسوأ (1) what is worse /   يدفع رسوماً   pay fees
مـن الـعار أن (2) It is shameful /   مـعظم   most of
يضطرون للقيام بأعمال شاقة have to do hard jobs
نحل solve /   ليس عدلاً   unfair   / مشكلة خطـيرة serious problem /
donate(3) يبرع بـ / governments (4) الـحكومات / ignore (5) تتجاهل
has the right له الحق في /   a sense of injustice (6) احساس بالـظلم /
endanger (7) يعرَض للخطر / save ينقذ / protect يحـمي
crime (8) الـجريمة / act quickly نـتصرف بسرعة
relieve (9) نـخفـف من معاناة

172

Composition 79 / The Arabic language اللغة العربية

      I want to tell you about Arabic. Arabic is an important language . Arabic is the language of the Holy Qur'an . Thanks to the Holy Qur'an , Arabic has survived for many years. Millions of people speak this language . The United Nations is using Arabic . Arabic has many dialects , but we use standard Arabic in newspapers , on TV and on the radio. Arabic has given many words to other languages. Arabic has taken words from other languages. I advise you to improve your Arabic .It is easy to do that. You can listen to radio and TV programs . You can read newspapers and magazines. I hope that you will follow my advice. The spread of Islam fosters the spread of Arabic ; people who embrace Islam tend to learn Arabic so that they can understand Islam better and perform Islamic rites.

* Key words :

survived (1)   بقيت حية   /   improve   تحسّـن
The United Nations (2)   الأمم المتحدة
dialects (3)   لهجات   /   spread   انتشار
standard Arabic   اللغة العربية الفصحى
foster   يشجع   /   embrace (4)   يعتنق - يدخل في الدين tend
يميل إلى   /   perform (5)   يؤدي - يقوم بـ
Islamic rites (6)   الشعائر الإسلامية

....

Composition 80 / Wedding customs تـقاليـد الـزواج *** Write a composition about wedding customs in your country.**

I want to tell you about wedding customs in my country. My people are proud of their wedding customs . First , they celebrate a wedding with songs and popular dances. Men dance with swords and use fire-arms and fire-works to show their joy. Second , the bride wears a white dress to show that she is pure. Third , they decorate the bride's hands and feet with henna to make her more beautiful. Fourth , my people have   a party for men and another one for women. They don't allow men to mix with women. Fifth , they slay goats and sheep and prepare a big meal to which a big number of guests are invited. Sixth , we welcome well-wishers by burning incense to produce a nice smell . Seventh , the groom's friends usually help him with some of the wedding's costs. Finally , some rich people travel to another country to spend the honeymoon.

In short , my people , like others, have their own wedding customs . These customs have become part of our heritage. We follow these customs when we celebrate a wedding , but we take care that improper things are not done.

* Key words :

(1) proud of فخـور	/ celebrate (2) يـحتتفـل بـ
wedding العـرس	/ popular dances رقصات شعبيـة
sword (3) سيـف	/ fire-arms أسلحة ناريـة
bride (4) العـروس	/ decorate يزيـن - يجمّـل
allow يسـمح لـ / mix with يختـلط مـع	/ slay ينحـر
goats المـاعـز / sheep الخـراف	/ prepare (5) يجهّـز guest
(6) الضيـف / are invited يتـم دعـوتهـم	well-wishers
تكاليـف costs / نتبـع follow / المـهنـئون	
by burning عن طريـق حـرق / produce ينتج / smell رائـحة	
groom العريـس	honeymoon (7) شهـر العسـل

improper things أشياء غير لائقة

part of our heritage جزء من تراثنا

....

* مـلا حـظـة نـطـق : ١- بـراود / ٢- سيـليب ريـت / ٣- سـورد / ٤- برايـد / ٥- بري بيـر / ٦- قست / ٧- ذا هـني مـوون

Composition 81 / Healthy teeth الأسنان الصحية * Write a composition about " Healthy teeth."

I want to tell you about healthy teeth. It is important to have healthy teeth. If you have healthy teeth , you will enjoy life. You should do something to keep your teeth healthy. First , you should eat a balanced diet. This balanced diet gives you all the nutrients that your body needs. Second , it is wrong to eat too many sweets . Sweets spoil your teeth. Third , it is advisable that you have dairy products because they are rich in calcium which makes your teeth stronger. Fourth, it is necessary to brush your teeth regularly. You should use a good tooth-brush and good tooth-paste for this purpose. Fifth , you should take care of your gums because they hold your teeth. Healthy gums mean healthy teeth. Sixth , it is important to see your dentist twice a year. You should see the dentist even though you don't have a tooth-ache. Finally , you should protect your teeth from accidents . If you do a sport , you can use a mouth guard . If you are driving in a car , you have to use the seatbelt.

In short , it is important to have healthy teeth. But if you have healthy teeth , you should keep them healthy .

* Key words :

enjoy life تـستـمـتع بـالـحـيـاة / sweets الحلويات
a balanced diet (1) غـذاء متـوازن / spoil تـُـفـسد
keep your teeth healthy تحافظ على صحة أسنانك
nutrients (2) مـواد مـغـذ ية / It is advisable يُـنصح
calcium الكـا لسـيـوم / dairy products (3) مـنتجات الألبان
dentist طبيب أسنان / regularly (4) بـا نتظام
protect تـحـمـي / for this purpose (5) لـهـذا الغـرض take
care of يعتني بـ / gums (6) اللـثـة
even though (7) حتى وإن - على الرغم من

175

tooth- ache (8)   / ألم في الأسنان   mouth guard (9)   حافظ للأسنان

....

* مـلاحـظـة نـطـق : ١- أبا لانـسـد دايـت / ٢- نـيـو تـريـا نـتـس ٣-
ديـري بـرو دكـتـس / ٤- رق يـو لار لـي / ٥- فـو ذس بـيـر بـوس / ٦- قـمـز /
٧- إيـفـن ذو / ٨- تـوث إيـك / ٩ - مـاوث قـارد

Composititon 82 / A thank- you letter   رسالة شكر
* Write a letter thanking somebody for his warm reception.

Dear Mr. White ,

   I am pleased to write to you. I would like to thank you for giving me the honour of staying with your family during my visit to your country. I had a wonderful time . It was nice of you to show me most of the interesting places in your country. I was impressed by your courtesy and your warm reception. In fact , you made me feel at home .
   I hope that you can come to my country so that I can repay your hospitality . I urge you to give me the pleasure of welcoming you to my hospitable country.
   Thank you again .
   With best wishes from .... ,

                              Yours sincerely ,

                              Nasser Hamad

* Key words :
pleased سعيد   / I am pleased to ..... يسعدني أن   during
يقيم مع   stay with   يمنحني شرف give me the honour (2) / أثناء (1)

I had a wonderful time. قضيت وقتاً رائعاً
show me تريني   / I was impressed (3) . تأثرت
courtesy (4) مجاملة – لطف / warm reception (5) استقبال حار feel at home
يشعر بالألفة / repay يجازي   hospitality
urge (7) يحث / كرم الضيافة (6)   pleasure (8)
hospitable (9) مضياف   / متعة

Composition 83/ My eating habits عاداتي الغذائية
  * **Write a composition about your eating habits.**

I , like other people, have my own eating habits. My eating habits are
things that I have been doing for a long time as far as food is concerned . I have
three meals a day : breakfast , lunch and dinner. I wash my hands before and
after having the meal. I usually have bread , cheese and dates for my breakfast. I
have bread , cooked vegetables , salads and fruit for lunch . I also have meat and
fish from time to time . I have a light meal for dinner. I like to have fresh fruit
and vegetables because they are rich in vitamins. I prefer fish to meat because it
does not contain too much fat. I hate to drink Pepsi and Cola products because
they contain pepsin , a peptic substance taken from the pig's bowels . I hate fast
meals because they are harmful for health . Fast-food restaurants sell ' junk '
food. I prefer home- made food. I hate to eat too much following the golden
saying that one's stomach is not a dustbin. My eating habits are based on the
advice that the stomach is a hot- bed of disease.

  * **Key words :**

as far as food is concerned فيما يتعلق بالطعام
meals وجبات / before and after having .... قبل وبعد تناول
dates التمر / a light meal وجبة خفيفة
prefer ..... to .... (1) يفضّل ... على ..... / pig الخنزير
contain (2) يحتوي على / fat دهون
products (3) منتجات / pepsin مادة الببسين
peptic substance (4) مادة مهضمة / bowels (5) أمعاء
harmful ضارة / junk food (6) طعام بالٍ
the golden saying المقولة الذهبية / stomach (7) المعدة
dust-bin (8) سلة مهملات / based on (9) مستندة على

177

advice (10)   النصيحة / hot-bed مرتع /   disease (11)   المرض

---

* ملاحظة نطق : 1- بري فير /2- كُن تيـن / 3- برو دكتس
4- ببتك سابس تانس   5- با ولـز / 6- جـنك فود / 7- ستـو مك / 8-
دست بـن /9- بيـزد 10- أد قا يـس / 11- دي زيـز

Composition 84 / Money   الـمــال

* Write a composition about money.

Money is playing a very important part in our life. People need it to meet their daily needs . Money is good in itself , but the important thing is how you get it and how you spend it. Money is a noble means if used to realize noble ends. Money is something great if got legally. Ill-got money is pure evil that will be inevitably used to realize base , dirty ends.

It is unjustly said that money is the root of every evil.. If this is the case , money should be rejected . This is impossible. Sensible people cannot accept this saying . Money is not to blame . Man who has this money is to blame . Some corrupt people seek to get money by all means. These people swindle , embezzle , forge , or lie to get money. These corrupt people are the evil-doers. They love money so much that they use diry means to get it. It is these corrupt people who should be discovered and punished . It is these corrupt people who distort the purity of money It is necessary to uproot all forms of corruption.

Love of money is instinctive in Man. Some people have a moderate instinct for money , so they get it legally and honourably. Others have an extreme instinct for money ; their greed for money drives them to get it by all means. Money can ennoble Man if got and used well , but it can degrade Man if got and used dishonourably.

In short , it is important for everybody to get money , but they should get it through noble means. Money is a blessing that can change our life for the better if used well.

178

* Key words :

play an important part in   يـلعب دوراً هـامـاً في   in
itself في حد ذاته

spend   يـنفق   /   a noble means   وسيـلـة نبيلـة   realize (1)
noble ends   غايات نبيلة   /   يـحـقـق   legally (2)   بصورة شرعية   /   ill-got money   مـا ل سـحت   pure evil
(3)   شـر سـرف   /   inevitably (4)   حـتـماً   base , dirty ends   root   جذر / أصل   غـايات دنيئة وقـذرة

if this is the case   إذا كـان الأمر هـكذا   /   uproot   يـقتلع – يخلع   /   يسعى
money should be rejected   الـمـا ل يـجب أن يُـنبـذ   /   seek
sensible   عاقل   /   accept (5)   يقبل بـ   this saying
هذا القول   /   Money is not to blame
المال لا يلام

corrupt (6)   فاسد   /   by all means   بكل وسيلة ممكنة   swindle
يـزور (تزوير)   forge (9)   يختلس   embezzle (8)   /   يحتال   (7)
/   blackmail (10)   يبتـز   lie   يكذب   /
should be discovered and punished   يجب أنْ يُفضحوا وُيعاقبوا   /
all forms of corruption (11)   جميع أشكال الفساد
distort   يشوه   /   purity (12)   صفاء – طهارة   instinct
(13)   غـريزه – فطرة   /   instinctive (14)   فطري   moderate   معتدل
/   extreme   متطرف
greed   جشع   /   ennoble   يسمو بـ
degrade   يحط من قدر   /   honourably (15)   بصورة شريفة
dishonourably   بصورة غير شريفة   /   blessing   نعمة
through (16)   من خلال – عن طريق

----

* ملاحظة نـطـق: ١- ريـا لايز / ٢- ليقا لي /٣- بـيور إيـثـل /   ٤- إن
إيـثـيـتابلي /٥- أك سبت / ٦- كـورا بت /٧- سـوين دل / ٨- إم بيـزل   /٩- فورج / ١٠-
بـلاك ميل / ١١ - كـوراب شن / ١٢- بـيو ريـتي

179

Composition 85 / The food problem مـشـكـلة الـغـذاء
* **Write a composition about this subject :**

" **Do you think there is a real food problem ?** "

I would like to express my opinion of the food problem. Millions of people are starving in many countries because they don't have enough food. Nobody can ignore this shameful situation. This serious problem should not exist because Allah guarantees food for everybody . Some countries produce big amounts of food and drop the surplus food into the sea. They are doing so on the pretext of keeping prices stable. It is shameful to hide food from hungry people . It is inhuman to have food while others are starving.

Some people allege that the increase in population is responsible for this starvation . This is not true . There is enough food in the world , but too few people are monopolizing this food , thus starving the majority of people. Islam rejects the monopoly of food . The monopoly of food is something disgraceful and should stop.

Starvation is a serious problem that should be quickly solved. The hungry can't wait for ever . Their problem should be solved , or else they will revolt for survival. The rich should realize this fact. The rich can solve the problem by ridding themselves of greed and egoism. It is true that the rich have the food and power , but they cannot use them to terrorize and silence the hungry. It is impossible for the rich to go on starving other people . Justice should prevail . Justice brings stability and peace. The haves should help the haven'ts . If this co-operation doesn't happen , wars will break out . The rich should realize that they can't enjoy security if the neighbours are starving.

In short , millions of people suffer from famines because selfish people are monopolizing food . The world is facing a serious food problem . The world has become insecure because wealth is monopolized by the minority. The well-fed minority have to stop starving other people ; hunger is a merciless enemy that people cannot tolerate .

* Key words :

starve (ستارڤ) ستجوْع - يموت جوعاً /

starvation (ستارڤيشن) الموت جوعاً - مجاعة - تجويع

ignore وضع - حالة - موقف (ست يوشن) situation / مخزي shameful

يتجاهل (إقنور) / serious (سير ياص) خطير

exist يكفل (قا رن تي) guarantee / يوج (إقزست)

produce كميات (أما ونتس) / ينتج (برود يوس) amounts

drop الفائض (سير بلاص) surplus / يُلقي - يرمي

on the pretext of بحجة - بذريعة / hide يُخفي

keep .... stable الحفاظ على استقرار / prices الأسعار

inhuman غير إنساني (إن هيوسن) / allege (أليج) يزعم

increase الزيادة (إنك ريس) /

population السكان (بوب يوليشن) / responsible for مسئولة عن monopolize

يحتكر (مونو بو لايز)

monopoly احتكار (مونو بولي) / majority (ماجو ريتي) الغالبية minority

الأقلية (مأينورتي) / reject يرفض

disgraceful مشين (دس قريس فل) / the hungry الجياع revolt for

survival (سير ڤأي ڤقال) يثورون من أجل البقاء

rid .... of يخلص (نفسه) من / greed الجشع

egoism الأنانية (أيقو وزم) / power السلطة

terrorize يرعب - يرهب (ترو رايز) silence (سأي لانس) justice يُسْكت

stability (سـتا) يسود (بري ڤيـل) prevail / العدل (جس تس)

co-operation الإستقرار (بيليتي) / the haves من يملكون

wars break out التعاون (كا أبا ريشن) realize / يدرك (ريا لايز)

security الحروب تندلع /

neighbours الأمن - الأمان (سك يورتي) /

insecure مجاعة (فا من) famine / الجيران (نيبا رز) (إن سك يور)

wealth الثروة (ولث) hunger الجوع (هتقر) / غير أمن

merciless عدو (إني مي) enemy لا يرحم (مير س لس) / tolerate

يتسامح مع (تولي ريت)

181

Composition 86 / Is it possible to quit smoking ?

* Write a composition about this subject : It is possible to quit smoking? هـل يمـكن تـرك الـتـدخـيــن ؟

I would like to express my opinion of smoking. Nobody can deny that smoking is bad for health. Smoking can cause serious diseases , so it is right for smokers to give it up. The question is : can a smoker give up smoking?

I think that smoking is not too difficult a problem to solve . Smoking is a very serious problem , but it can be solved. First , a smoker has to realize that cigarettes endanger his health ; cigarettes can cause a smoker fatal diseases. The smoker is destroying his life , so he has to think of a way-out. He has to quit smoking to survive . Second , smoking is a habit one acquires from others , so it is easy to give it up. Third , one can give up smoking if he has a strong will. If there is a will , there is a way. It is important to possess the determination to resist the temptation of a cigarette . If there is this determination , one can move mountains. Fourth , cigarettes cost one too much money , money that one should spend on what benefits him and his children. Finally , one has to give up smoking for the sake of his children. If a parent smokes , children will follow his (her) example. The parent has to set a good example for children.

In short , smoking is harmful , so it is wise to give it up. It is not difficult to do that. All that one needs is the strong will . Remember that one can perform miracles if there is a will.

* Key words :

quit (1)   يقلع عن   /   give up   يترك
serious   خطير   /   endanger   تعرّض للخطر
ليست   not too difficult a problem to solve

بالمشكلة الصعبة التي لا تُحل

has to realize   عليه أن يدرك   /   can cause   يمكن أن تسبب   fatal diseases
(2)   أمراض مميتة   /   destroy   يدمر   for the
sake of   من أجل   /   think of a way out   يفكّر في مخرج
survive (3)   ينجو – يبقى على قيد الحياة   /   a habit   عادة   one (4)
المرء   /   acquire (5)   يكتسب
others (6)   /   will   إرادة
possess (7)   يمتلك   /   benefit   يفيد
determination (8)   التصميم – العزيمة   /   resist (9)   يقاوم   spend   ينفق
cost   تكلف   temptation (10)   إغراء   /

It is wise to .....   من الحكمة أن   perform
miracles (11)   يصنع معجزات   set a good example
يضرب المثل الأعلى – يكون قدوة

----

*ملاحظة نطق : ١- اكويت / ٢- فيتا ل ديزيزز /٣- سير ڤا يڤ
/ ٤- وان / ٥- أكوا يار / -٦ أذا رز / ٧- بوز يس /
٨- دي تير مينيشن / ٩- ري زيست / -١٠ تمبي تيشن /
-١١ بَر فورم ميرا كالز .

183

Composition 87 / The Satellite TV Channels   قنوات

التــلــفـزة الـفـضائـية

* **Write a composition about the satellite TV channels.**

    I would like to draw the attention to the remarkable role played by the satellite TV channels. Thanks to modern technology , satellite TV channels have emerged and flourished making information accessible to everybody wherever they are . Nobody can ignore that the satellite TV channels have given a great boost to the mass media . First , they have put an end to the state- controlled information , thus giving validity to the role of free information. Second , they have removed barriers to the smooth exchange of information, which brings the globe's peoples closer. In this way , they can create a common world opinion regarding important issues . Third , they report events simultaneously so that they keep the viewers in touch with world events . Fourth , they have encouraged freedom of expression and made it clear that this freedom is one of Man's basic rights . Fifth , the satellite TV channels have made the world a small village , thus creating   a universal interest in world affairs. Sixth, these channels give people free access   to a new kind of information completely different from the misleading state-controlled media . Thanks to them , people have become better-informed and consequently in a far better position to assess matters.   Finally , people have discovered   how misleading the state-controlled media are , which shows the falling number of the latter's viewers.

    In brief , the satellite TV channels have become popular with a big number of people   deriving   their popularity   from their credibility and reliability. Thanks to them , to mislead people is no longer possible ; in fact , misleading has become out-dated. Survival is for the fittest!

184

● Key words :

satellite channels (1)   القنوات الفضائية   /   emerged (2)   بـرزت
draw the attention to   يلفت الإنتباه إلى   /   flourished (3)   ازدهـرت
information   الإعلام – المعلومات   /   accessible (4)   سهـل المنال
boost (5)   دفعة   /   mass media (6)   وسائل الإعلام put an end to
وضع حداً لـ   /   removed   أزالت
state-controlled   الـمسيطر عليه من قبل الدولة
barriers (7)   الـحواجـز   /   report events   ينقل الأحداث
smooth exchange (8)   التبادل السلس / misleading   مضللة – تضليل globe's
peoples   شعوب العالم   /   create   يخلق
a common world opinion   رأي عالمي مشترك   encourage (9)   يشجع
basic rights   /   regarding   فيما يتعلق بـ   /
simultaneously (11)   في نفس اللحظة / latter   الأخير world affairs   شئون عالمية   /   الحقوق الأساسي (10)
universal interest   اهتمام عالمي   /   discover   يكتسف
keep.... in touch with   تبقى ... على صلة بـ
give ..... access to (12)   تـعطي ... نافذة إلى   /   derive   تستمد
validity (13)   صـلاحية – مـصداقية   /   credibility (14)   مصداقية
reliability (15)   الثقة   /   better-informed   ويتم إعلامه بشكل أفضل a new kind of
information   نوع جديد من الإعلام
position (16)   وضع   /   assess (17)   يقيّم
viewer (18)   المشاهد   /   falling number (19)   عدد آخذ في الهـبوط   popular with
out-dated   مهـمل   popularity (20)   شعبية   /   مـحبوبة لدى
survival for the fittest (21)   الدور البارز   remarkable role   /
البـقاء للأصـلح

----

* ملاحظة نطـق : 1- ستا لايت تشا نلز / 2- إميـرجد / 3- فلا رشد   4-
أكسيـسي بل / 5- بـوو سـت / 6- مـاس ميد يا / 7- بار يارز   8- سموذ إكس
تشينج / 9- إنكا رج / 10- بيـزك رايتس / 11- سيـما ل تا ن ياصلي /
12- أكسيس   13/ - فا ليديتي / 14- كريدي بيليتي / 15- ري ليا
بيليتي / 16- بـوزيشن

185

Composition 88 / A sea disaster   كـا رثـة بـحـريــة   * **Write a**
composition about a sea disaster you witnessed or
  heard of.

  " The Noble " is a passenger ship that usually travelled between East African and South Asian ports. One day, the ship set off carrying five hundred passengers apart from the crew. The weather conditions were perfect ; there were no strong winds or waves. Visibility was excellent and the weather was sunny.

  Two hours later , the weather suddenly changed for the worse when most of the passengers were on the deck enjoying the beautiful view of the sea. A storm hit the ship mercilessly. The passengers panicked and began to pray for safety. There was a state of panic and confusion. The crew tried in vain to pacify the passengers. The captain asked everybody to follow the safety instructions. The crew gave the passengers life-jackets and showed them how to use the safety-boats.

  The storm was getting worse . The captain sent an SOS message . The ship was in trouble , so he had to call for help. The captain asked everybody to act wisely . Unluckily ,   the captain lost control because of bad visibility . Some of the passengers threw themselves into the sea and swam for safety. The ship capsized and sank , so many passengers drowned.

  Some helicopters soon arrived and started a rescue operation. They pulled some survivors . The coastguard boats saved some people. Other ships in the area helped with the rescue operation. Many dead bodies were pulled .

  It was a real disaster , but who was to blame for it ? The disaster took place because of merciless , bad weather conditions. There was no human fault. Nobody is to blame for natural disasters.

* Key words :

passenger ship	سفينة للركاب	/	موانئ ports
set off	بدأت رحلة	/	carry يحمل
apart from	بالإضافة إلى	/	crew (1) الطاقم
weather conditions	الأحوال الجوية	/	visibility

الرؤية (2)

excellent (3)	ممتاز	/	view of the deck سطح السفينة
sea (4)	منظر البحر	/	storm عاصفة

mercilessly (5)   بلا رحمة

panicked (6)   أصيبوا بالذعر

a state of panic (7)   حالة من الذعر

confusion (8)   الإرتباك

in vain   دون جدوى

pacify (9)   يهدئ من روع

life-jackets   سترات النجاة

SOS message   إشارة استغاثة

act wisely   يتصرف بحكمة   /   capsized (10) إنقلبت   sank غرقت

rescue operation (11) عملية   drown يغرق   /

انقاذ   /   survivors (12) الناجون coastguard boats (13) قوارب خفر السواحل

/   blame يلوم

Who is to blame ?   من يتحمل المسؤلية

human fault (14)   خطأ بشري

natural disaster (15)   كارثة طبيعية

----

* ملاحظـة نـطـق : ١- كـرو / ٢- فـزي بيليتي -٣
إكسي لانت /٤- فـيو / ٥- ميرس لسلي /٦- با نكد   -٧ أستيت أق
با نك / ٨- كـونـف يوجن / ٩- با سي فاي   -١٠ كـا ب سا يـزد / ١١- رس
كيو أبا ريـشن   -١٢ سيـر فـاي فـا رز /١٣- كـوست قـا رد
بوتـس   -١٤ هيـو مـن فـولت / ١٥- نـا تشرال دي زاس
تـا ر

187

Composition 89 / A plane crash   تحطم طائرة

An Armenian plane took off from Yurevan Airport heading for
Moscow Airport with two hundred passengers and a seven-man crew aboard .
Everything was perfect ; weather conditions were not bad. An hour later , the
captain received   a call from the
control tower at Moscow Airport , telling him
that bad weather conditions did not allow the plane to land at Moscow Airport.
The captain had to change his destination , so he headed for the nearest airport.
Half an hour later , he received another call , telling him that weather conditions
improved . The captain changed his direction , heading for Moscow Airport.
When the plane approached Moscow Airport , it started to slow down   ,
preparing for landing. By that time , the fuel had run out ! Before the plane
could reach the runway , it landed on a near-by building . The plane crashed ,
and all the passengers were killed. The building was partly damaged , and five
people were killed and fifteen injured.

Rescue operations soon started. Fire-men began to put out the fire. The
rescuers carried the injured people to a near-by hospital . The dead people were
taken to other hospitals. The debris was removed , and the traffic police acted
quickly to ease traffic .

This is a real disaster . I blame both the captain and the air controllers at Moscow Airport. If they had acted well , the disaster would not have happened. I feel sorry for the victims , hoping that similar disasters will not happen in the future .

* Key words :

took off   أقلعت   متوجهة إلى heading for /

crew (1)   طاقم   على متنها aboard/

weather conditions   الظروف الجوية / received a call تلقى مكالمةcontrol tower برج

المراقبة   يلوم blame /

allow   تسمح لـ   وجهته destination / approached (2)

اقتربت من   preparing for / استعداداً run out لم يبقى منه شيئاً – نفد

fuel (3) الوقود /

runway   مـدرج المطار   / rescue operations (4) عمليات الانقاذrescuers

نقلوا carried /   المسعفون

the injured (5)   المصابين   / debris (6) الأنقاض

removed تم إزالة   / ease يسهّل

disaster (7) كارثة   / air controllers المراقبون victims (8) الضحايا

نـقطة نـطـق : ١- كرو / ٢- أب روتشد / ٣- فيـو ل /
٤ - رسكيو أبو و ريشنز / ٥- ذي إنجا ارد / ٦- دب ري

189

Composition 90 / An Air Piracy قـرصـنـة جـويـة
* **Write a composition about this topic: " a fearful experience you had , but it ended well."**

It was five o'clock in the afternoon when I boarded   a Qatari Airliner. The plane took off from Doha Airport heading for Amman. Half an hour later , a passenger approached the cockpit , knocking nervously at the door . He shouted at the pilot asking him to change the direction of the plane. He threatened to explode the plane if he faced any resistance. I thought it was a hijacking attempt. The passengers panicked and expected that a disaster would take place. They were worried . The security men asked the passengers to keep quiet . The security men acted cleverly. They talked to the hijacker and promised to meet his demands. While they were talking , some security men took the hijacker by surprise . They hit him on the head , knocking him down. As soon as the hijacker fell , the security men arrested him . They handcuffed him and took away the gun that he was holding. Order was soon restored . The passengers were relieved when the operation ended safely. Nobody was hurt and the disaster did not take place. It was a fearful flight , but I thanked Allah that the security men foiled the hijacking operation. Everybody aboard the plane felt

relieved that the hijacking attempt failed . It was a terrible experience because

human lives were in real danger , but relief soon came when the attempt ended

safely.

* Key words :

board a plane طائرة ركاب يصعد على الطائرة / airliner
head for يتوجه إلى / cockpit قمرة approach (1) يقترب من
الطيار / knock (2) يخبط
nervously بعصبية / direction يصرخ shout
إتجاه / threaten (3) يهدد
explode يفجّر / hijack (5) مقاومة resistance (4)
يحطف طائره / hijacking attempt محاولة اختطاف
panicked أصيبوا بالذعر / expected توقعوا
disaster (6) كارثة / acted cleverly (7) تصرفوا بذكاء meet his
demands يلبي مطالبه took .... by surprise (8)
باغت
arrested ألقوا القبض على
handcuff (9) يكبل اليدين
order النظام / restored تم استعادة
relieved شعروا بالإرتياح / operation (10) العملية a fearful
flight (11) رحلة مخيفة / security الأمن
foiled أحبطوا / aboard على متن الطائرة failed فشلت
/ experience تجربة
human lives (12) أرواح بشرية / relief (13) الفرج
piracy (14) قرصنة

----

* ملاحظة نطق : ١- أب روو تش / ٢- نوك / ٣- ثريتن ٤- ريز
يس تا نس / ٥- هاي جاك / ٦- دي زاس تار ٧- أكتد كليقا ر
لي / ٨- توك باي سير برايز / ٩- هاند كف ١٠- أبا ريشن / ١١- أفير
فل فلايت / ١٢ - هيومن لايقز ١٣ - ريليف / ١٤- باي راسي

191

Composition 91 / A self- made man رجــل عـصـامـي

Wtite a story of a man who could overcome many obstacles to make himself a fortune.

أكتـب قـصة رجــل اسـتطاع أن يـتغـلب على عـقبات كثيرة ليكوْن لنفسه ثـروة .

      Hassan was born in a village in 1920. His parents had   a tiny piece of land . They were farmers who lived a very simple life. The parents died of cholera when Hassan was only six years old. Hassan 's uncle took care of him. The uncle was too poor to send Hassan to school , so he decided to teach Hassan how to be a farmer. At first , the idea appealed to Hassan , but two years later , Hassan chose to do something different. He begged his uncle to send him to school. The uncle was so kind to Hassan that he let Hassan have his desire.

      Hassan joined a primary school in his village . The uncle had to borrow the fees from a well-off villager. Hassan worked hard and got the best marks at school , so the school decided to relieve him of the fees. The uncle was impressed by Hassan's progress , so he encouraged Hassan to study harder . At the age of 18 , Hassan passed the exams of the secondary education with top marks , so he joined the medical college . The government decided to pay for Hassan's education. That encouraged Hassan to make more successes. Six years later , Hassan got his medical degree , setting a good example for the young villagers .

      Hassan's story of success is important because it became a source of inspiration for the young villagers . Thanks to Hassan's story , the number of the educated villagers rose remarkably.

* Key words :

took care of   قطعة أرض صغيرة (1) a tiny piece of land

too poor to send ....   رعى – اعتنى به   فقير
      جداً بحيث لم يتمكن من إرسال

chose   اختار   راقت له appealed to him /   قرر (2) decided

well-off   /   التحق بـ joined   توسل لـ begged /
ثري

let ..... have his desire   ترك ... يحقق رغبته

relieve him of (3)   تعفيه من

progress   had to borrow the fees   اضطر أن يستدين الرسوم

(4) تقدم   /   encouraged (5)   شجع

set a   medical college (6) كلية الطب

good example لـ يضرب المثل الأعلى

make more   story of success (7) قصة نجاح

successes يحقق المزيد من النجاح   the young

villagers الشباب القرويون   became a

source of inspiration (8) أصبحت مصدر الهام

ملاحظة نطق : ١- أتاي ني بيس .... / ٢- دي ساي دد / ٣- ريليق
٤- برو قرس / ٥- إنكا رجد / ٦ - ميدي كال كو ليج   ٧- سك سس
/ ٨- أسورس أڤ إنس بي ريشن

193

Composition 92 / A fearful experience I will never forget .

تجربة مروعة لن أنساها

Let me tell you a fearful experience that I will never forget.   I used to live in a small village on Java Island of Indonesia. One day ,   I was having breakfast with my family. Outside , the weather was fine and everything was quiet . Suddenly , a very strong earthquake hit the island , destroying houses and hotels and sending hysterical people running into the   streets. The earthquake cracked the ground , burying thousands of people alive . The earthquake caused big cracks in the ground , sending fearful tidal   waves everywhere. The tidal waves soon reached our village , flooding houses and roads and killing thousands of people. People panicked and ran to hills and mountains for safety. Some people left their homes , leaving children behind. Many ships and boats were destroyed. The coastal areas   were hard- hit. Thousands of people were homeless .

The situation was awful. Thousands of   corpses were lying everywhere , making the spread of epidemics imminent . The survivors were in real trouble . They had nothing to eat or drink. Many people did not know what happened to their children. Nobody could help because roads and airports were badly damaged. Roads and bridges were   destroyed , hindering   rescue operations. Rescue teams pulled bodies from the   rubble and people   began digging mass graves.The survivors badly needed help , or else they would perish . Something had to be done to avoid another disaster .   It was such a fearful experience that it is not easy to forget .

* Key words :

Java Island (1)   جزيرة جاوه   /   earthquake (2)   زلزال

hysterical (3)   المصابون بهستيريا

سبب انكسارات   cracked

bury ..... alive (4)   يدفن......أحياءً   /   tidal waves   أمواج المد flood (5)

التلال   hills   أصيبوا بالذعر   panicked   /   يغمر بالمياه

طلباً للأمان   for safety   /

coastal areas   المناطق الساحلية   /   hard-hit   تضررت كثيراً situation (6)

الوضع   corpse (7)   جثة   /

the spread of epidemics (8)   انتشار الأوبئة

imminent   وشيكاً   /   survivors (9)   الناجون   in real

trouble (10)   في محنة حقيقية

hinder   يعيق   /   dig   يحفر

rescue operations (11)   عمليات الإغاثة   /   pulled   قاموا بانتشال

lying   ملقاة   /   rubble (12)   الأنقاض

mass graves   قبور جماعية   /   perish (13)   يهلكوا

ملاحظة نطق : ١- جاڤا أي لاند / ٢- إيرث كويك

٣- هس تيري كال / ٤- باري .... ألا يڤ / ٥- فلا د

٦- ست يو ويشن / ٧- كورس / ٨- إبدي مكس

٩- سير ڤاي ڤارز / ١٠- إن ريال ترابل

١١- رسكيو أبا ريش / ١٢- رابل / ١٣- بريش

195

Proverbs حـكـم

A proverb expresses in a few words a truth that relates to everday experience and has a universal value.

الـحكمة تعبّركلمات قليلة عن حقيقة ترتبط بتجربة يومية ولها قيمة عالمية.

* Brevity is the soul of wit.

الإختصار عبادة . (إن الإختصار في اللغة دليل على ذكاء الشخص)

* Charity begins at home.

الأقـربـون أولى بـالـمـعـروف .

* Still water runs deep.

تحت السواهي دواهي .

* Too many hands spoil the broth.

كثرة الـطـبـاخـيـن تـفـسد الطبخة .

* Prevention is better than cure.

الـوقـايـة خير من العلاج .

* Blood is thicker than water.

الدم لا يصبح ماءً .

* Ink is better than the strongest memory.

العلم في القرطاس وليس في الرأس .

* When your home is made of glass , don't throw stones at others.

إذا كان بيتك من زجاج فلا ترشق الأخرين بالحجارة . (إذا كان بك عيوباً , فلا تنتقد الأخرين.)

* The Englishman's home is his castle.

بيت الإنجليزي قلعته .

* Deeds are better than the strongest words.

الأفعال لا الأقوال . / النص نص علماء والفعل فعل شياطين.

* Cleanliness is next to godliness.

النظافة من الإيمان .

* In much wisdom is much much grief.

المجانين في نعيم والعقلاء في جحيم.

* When you have reached 40 , a new ailment is suffered each
  year.

عندما يصل بك العمر إلى سـن الأربعين تصبح عرضة لعلة جديده كل عام.

* Climb like a cucumber, fall like an aubergine.

تـسـلّـق مثل الخيارة وانزل مثلا الباذنجانة. (سر بحذر تضمن السلامة.)

* To lick the sky with the tongue is to cry for the moon.

من ينظر فوق تنكسر رقبته.

* When the mother and father are weeds , how can the
  daughter be a saffron   root?

اسحب البنت من كمها تطلع البنت لأمها . (إذا كان رب البيت للدف ضارباً , فشيمة أهل
البيت الـطبـل والـرمـر.)

* Too soft and you will be squeezed; too hard and you will be
  broken.

لا تكن ليْناً فـتـعصر , ولا تكن صلباً فتكسر .

* Better to ride a dung- beetle than tread on soft carpets.

أفضل لك أن تركب خنفساءً من أن تسير على سجاد ناعم.

* An intelligent enemy is better that an ignorant friend.

عـدو عاقل خيـر من صديق جاهل.

* To teach the bride , beat the cat.

لكي ترهب العروس إقتل أمامها قطة.

" خـوّف صـاحـبـك , يـحـسـب لك حـساب. "

* Every man is a child in his own home.

كل إمرءٍ يقطّن في قطينه

* You have baked your own bread ; it is yours and that of your
  children.

عملك لك ولأولادك (عملك مردود عليك.)

* As you make your bed , so you must lie in it.

طابخ السم لابد أنه أكل منه.

* It is better to endure the wind of a camel than the prayers of a
  fish.

نار ..... ولا نعيم ......

* No gains without pains.

كل شيئ بثمن . (ما فيش شيئ ببلاش الا العمى والطراش)

* Not all that glitters is gold.

ليس كل ما يلمع ذهباً .

*Speech is silver , Silence is golden .

إذا كان
الكلام من فضة , فالسكوت من ذهب.

* Never put off till tomorrow what you can do today.

لا تؤجل عمل اليوم للغد.

* More haste ,
less speed.

في التأني السلامة , وفي العجلة الندامة

* If ignorance is bliss , it is folly to be wise.

إذا كانت السعادة في الجهل , فمن الحمق أن نسعى إلى الحكمة .

* Half a loaf is better than nothing.

رائحة البر أفضل من عدمه .

* Birds of the feather fly together.

إن الطيور على أشكالها تقع .

* A friend in need is a friend indeed.

الصديق في
وقت الضيق هو الصديق حقاً.

* Many hands make light work.

" يد على
يد رحمة ."الحمل إذا توزع ينشال."
" الحمل على الجماعة ريش."

*Two heads are better than one. ما خاب من استشار

* A bird in the hand is worth two in the bush.

عصفور باليد ولا إثنين فوق الشجرة.

* A stitch in time saves nine. "أضرب على الحديد وهو حامي. "

* Learn to walk before you run. اصعد السلم درجة درجة.

* When in Rome , do as the Romans do.

يا غريب خليك أديب. أرْضهم ما دمت في أرْضهم .

* Faith can move mountains . بالإيمان تزول الصعاب .

* Don't count your chickens before they are hatched. ليس بيدك ما إلي

لك .

" لا تحسب كتاكيتك قبل حدوث التفقيس ."

* The early bird catches the worm. الذي

يسبق يأكل النبق . " إلى سبق أخذ النبق."

* No news is good news. القوم بخير طالما لا يرد منهم خبر .

* When the cat's away , the mice will play.

غاب القط , العب يا فار .

* Obey the

dog in authority. أطعْ الكلب الذي بيده

السلطة.

بوس الكلب على فمه لما تاخد غرضك منه."

* Man proposes and God disposes. الإنسان في

التفكير و الله في التدبير.

199

The Index   الـفـهـرس

The Author's Biography
سيـرة المـؤلـف

* Born in Palestine in 1946.   . وُلـد في فلسـطيـن عام ١٩٤٦

* Joined Cairo University in 1963 and majored in
English language and literature with grade " Good".

التحـق بجامعة القاهرة عام ١٩٦٣ وحصل على درجة الليسانس بتقدير "
جيد".

* Has been a teacher of English with Qatar's Ministry of
education since 1967.

يعمـل مـدرسـاً لـلـغـة الإنجليزية في وزارةالتربيـةوالتعـليم
القطرية منذ العـام ١٩٦٧ .   Sent to *
Britain in 1969 on an in-service training course
that focused on teaching English as a second language.

أرسـل إلى بـريـطانـيـا في دورة تدريبية موضوعها تدريس الإنجليزية
كلغة ثانية.

* Obtained an Education Diploma in teaching English as a second language
from Qatar University in 1977.

حصـل على دبلـوم في التربية وطرق تدريس الإنجليزية كلغة ثانية من جامعة قطر عـام
.١٩٧٧

* Attended several seminars and training courses in Qatar.

حـضـر عـدة دورات تدريبية وحلقات دراسية عـقـدت بقطر   Has *
published four books :   قـا م بـنـشـر أربـعـة مـؤلـفـات

The Sound Approach to English Grammar.

الـطـريـقـة المـثلى لقواعد اللـغة الإنجليزيـة

English for Beginners.

اللـغـة الإنجـلـيـزيـة للمبتدئيـن

Art of Writing.   فـن الـكـتـا بـة

A Simplified English – Arabic Glossary of Words in
Use.

القـا موس المـبـسّط إنجليزي – عربي لكلمات متداولة.

205

تـقديـم

أقـدّم هـذا الـقاموس المبسّط بهـدف تزويد الراغبين في تنمية قدراتهم في اللغة الإنجليزية بكلمات متداولة ومطلوبة بإلحاح كبير تمكّن الدارس من القيام بتواصل فعّال مع الأخـرين.

ونظراً لأهمية النطق السليم للكلمة فإنني حاولت قدر الإمكان رسم صوتي للكلمة الإنجليزية بأحرف عربية . وبما أن لغة الضاد تحتل مكاناً فريداً بين اللغات , فقد وجدت صعوبة كبيرة في نقل الصوت من الإنجليزية إلى العربية. وبناءً على هذا , رأيت أن أعطي مفتاحاً صوتياً لعله يساعد على تقريب النطق .

و بد من الإشارة إلى أن احتكاك الدارس بالناطقين الإصليين للغة أفضل وسيلة للحصول على النطق السليم للكلمة . كما أنني أريد التنويه إلى وجود اختلافات كبيرة في النطق بين الإنجليز والأمريكان خاصة فيما يتعلق بحرف " r" . فالإنجليز على عكس الإمريكان لا يميلون إلى نطقه في حالات كثيرة .

Introduction

This simplified glossary is aimed at providing people willing to develop their English with words that are commonly used and urgently needed , thus enabling the learner to communicate effectively with others.

Due to the importance of sound pronunciation , I tried hard to produce an Arabic transcription of the English word. Since Arabic is a unique language , I found it difficult to transcribe an English word in Arabic letters. Therefore , I am supplying a phonetic key that may help give the learner an approximate transcription of the English word.

It is worth saying that the best way to pronounce a word correctly is to mix with the native speakers of English. I would like to stress the fact that there are big differences in pronunciation between the Englishmen and the Americans ; particularly the phone " r " . The Englishmen , unlike the Americans , do not pronounce this phone in many cases.

Phonetic Key

a man / مان / (آ)
main / مين / (إيه)
late / ليت / (إيه)
play / بلي / (إيه)
ball / بو:ل / (و:)
cause / كو:ز / (و :)

e ten / تِنْ / (ي)
seen / سين / (ي:)

i fine / فاين / (أي)
wife / وايف , like / لايك /
win / ون / (ي)
hit / هـت , ring / رنق /
bird / بيرد / (أير)
girl (قيرل) , first / فيرست /
fight / فايت / (أي)

o hot / هُـت / (و)
soon / سوون / (وو)

u use / يوز- يوس / (يو)
pure / بيو(ر) /

up / أب / (أ)
under / أن د(ر) /

queen / كوين / (وي)

trouble (أ) / ترا بل /
harbour / هار بر /
country / كن تري
turn / تيرن / (إيـر)
hurt / هـيرت /

picture (تشَ) / (ر) بك تش /

c (ك) can / كان /
clock / كلوك /

pencil (س) / بن سل /
centre / س تر /
decency / دي سن سي /

cia (شَ) social / سو شل /
cie (ش) efficient / إفِ شنت /
cio (ش) delicious / ديلي شص /

ch (تش) cheap / تشيب /
rich / رتش /
ch (ش) branch / برانش /
ch (ك) chemist / كيمست /
chord / كورد /

g (ق) get / قِت /
(ج) gentle / جن تل /
gh (.) light / لايت /
gh (ف) laugh / لاف /
s (س) sit / ست /
rise (ز) / رايز /

sh (ش) ship / شب /

/ كوا ليـتي / quality

/ كـويك / quick

/ كويست / quest

/ فاوند / (أو) found

f (ف) fan / فان /

v (ڤ) van / ڤان /

h (هـ) him / هِمْ /

hat / هـات /

th (ذ) this / ذس /

thank (ث) / ثا نك /

sio (ج) vision / في جن /

tension (ش) / تن شن /